DON'T JUST BREAK THROUGH

BREAK FREE!

Puah Neiel

But you are a chosen race, a royal priesthood, a holy nation, a people for His own possession, that you may proclaim the excellencies of Him who called you out of darkness into his marvelous light. 1Peter 2:9.

DON'T JUST BREAK THROUGH, BREAK FREE!

By Puah Neiel

Publisher: Healing Balm Cafe Books, LLC

Post Office Box 154

New York, NY 10027 U.S.A

Website: www.Healingbalmcafe.com

Email: Healingbalmcafe@gmail.com

All rights reserved. No part of this book may be reproduced or transmitted in any form or by any means, electronic or mechanical, including the internet, photocopying, recording, translating or by any information storage and retrieval system, without written permission from the author, except for the inclusion of brief quotations, giving credit solely to the author.

All Bible verses are taken from NKJV unless otherwise noted.

Copyright © 2017 by Healing Balm Cafe Books, LLC.

ISBN Numbers: 10: 0-9963126-2-5   13: 978-0-9963126-2-2

First Edition 2016. Printed in the United States of America

Library Of Congress Cataloging-in-Publication Data:

Don't Just Break Through, BREAK FREE! By Puah Neiel.

Control Number: 2015906168

Book Cover Design: Exodus Design

Disclaimer

This book is designed to provide information regarding Bible study, prayer, and the Christian lifestyle. It is sold with the agreement that the publisher and author are not providing counseling, pastoral or health advice or services. If spiritual guidance or counseling is needed, the services of a Christian counseling professional or pastoral clergy should be sought.

You are urged to read the available material, follow its recommendations, and tailor the information according to your individual needs. With a willingness to learn and diligent study habits, the goals of this book can be obtained.

Every effort has been made to ensure that this text is as accurate as possible. However, there may be mistakes, both typographical and in content. Therefore this book should be used as a general guide and not a replacement for daily Bible reading.

The author and Healing Balm Cafe Books, LLC shall neither be held liable or responsible to any person or entity for the information contained in this book.

Dedication

I would like to dedicate this book to the hurting, broken, and hopeless. I've found my way out of the dark tunnel, so I pass this torch on to you. It was once said, *"We don't find books, books find us!"* I pray that this book finds you at your darkest hour; as a guiding light on your spiritual journey. Though you may not be able to see the end, be encouraged, there is a way out!

CONTENTS

	DISCLAIMER	iv
	DEDICATION	v
	INTRODUCTION	ix
1	Poem: FREE	1
2	Thank You!	3
3	Prayer	9
4	Healing Balm Cafe: The Introduction	13
5	God Is Love	15
6	Felt Like Giving up Lately?	18
7	An Evening At The Healing Balm Cafe	28
8	God, If You Are Real...	32
9	God, Where Are You?	37
10	Be Still And Know That I Am God	63
	-God's Love	64
	-God's Voice	65
	-God's Presence	66
11	The Wedding	71
12	The Love Train	74
13	What Is My Calling?	76

14	A Soliloquy Of Love's Consuming Fire: In Four Acts	81
15	Christian Seasons	83
16	Healing Balm Cafe's 10 Commandments	92
17	A Mother's Love	96
18	The Funeral	98
19	Gospel*mercial*	100
20	If The Bible Is A Sword...Fasting Is A Battle Axe	102
21	Meditate On The Word	111
22	Healing Balm Cafe: The Eulogy	116
23	God's Classifieds	122
24	Life Vs. Death	124
25	Soldier In The Army	127
26	Granny Gospel Wisdom	130
27	I Am Weak, Yet I Am Strong	132
28	Is Your Spiritual House Dirty?	142
29	Natural Organic Mood Lifter	147
30	1-800-J-E-S-U-S	150
31	The Devil Answers Prayers Too	155
32	The Game	163

33	I Gave Up Religion And Went Back To Drinking	165
34	Healing Balm Cafe: Is your food making you sick?	170
35	It's Not A Person Harassing You, It's A Spirit	174
36	Who's Tied To Your Soul?	181
37	Your Garden of Gethsemane	188
	-God is teaching you to worship Him	191
	-Has God called you to serve in ministry?	193
	-Is it persecution or spiritual maturing?	195
38	Your Worst Enemy	198
39	Does Persecution Mean God Is Punishing Me?	205
40	The Valley Of The Shadow Of Death	211
41	The Red Pumps	219
	-Accepting Jesus as your Savior	223
	-Christian tools	226
	- Tithing	231
	-Communion	232
42	On The Road To Salvation	233
43	From God, With Love	239
44	Elizabeth Kublet-Ross Quote	243

Introduction

Are you ready to be permanently set free from bad habits, addictions, negative thinking, impulsive behavior? Are you ready to learn how to be a powerful Christian instead of a defeated one? This book is the answer to your prayers! How many times have you been delivered from strongholds or sin in your life, and after a short time later you're once again held captive or enslaved to the very thing that you escaped from? Yes, you may have prayed. Yes, you may have changed your life style. Yes, you may have sought counseling. But until you understand that this is a spiritual problem (regardless of the situation) and not a physical one, you will continually be bound. Meaning, you must learn the necessary tools to attack the problem spiritually; therefore, annihilating it permanently!

The Bible says in Matthew 12:43-45, that when an unclean spirit leaves a person, it goes out walking the earth seeking a new home. Beloved, if you are not continually doing the thing that chased the spirit out of your life in the beginning, have yet learned the tools of spiritual warfare, or have left a door ajar to sin; Matthew 12:44-45, says this same spirit will not only return to its home, but bring with it seven even more diabolical spirits, and the person will be worse off in the latter than he was in the beginning. More, the person will be bound by these spirits until he or she learns how to break free for good!

You are now holding in your hand the chain breaker! ***Don't Just Break Through, BREAK FREE!*** Will teach you practical steps on how to identify, defeat, and eradicate stubborn problems, and give you the materials needed to study on a day-to-day basis, so that whenever an old habit does try to resurface in your life, you will have this handy reference available to help you when you're feeling weak and are attacked spiritually.

More, ***Don't Just Break Through, BREAK FREE!*** is a keepsake! It is a compilation of Biblical teaching, inspirational stories, poetry, humor, and preachin' that will encourage you right out of your spiritual rut! Keep a copy handy on a dresser, coffee table, work desk, in the car, or in your purse for a quick word of encouragement. It will take you on an uplifting journey that will have you laughing, crying, praying and praising, as you live vicariously through characters such as: *Agape Love, Grandma "Granny" Gospel, JC Reppa, and Phat Johnny.* With words of wisdom, humor, and sound teaching; your spirit will be lifted up way high by hilarious *Jesus* commercials, Christian infomercials and Christian jingles. Moreover, your soul will be stirred with inspirational teaching, *practical* and *relevant* Bible verses, short stories, and examples of historical figures who had an unbreakable will to survive!

In today's demanding and stressful world, it's easy to get off track, lose focus, and let discouragement become commonplace in your life; negating you of the joy that is inherently yours! At this very moment you may find yourself in a place devoid of happiness, joy, or even peace, asking as Elijah did in 2 Kings 2:14: "Where is the Lord God of Elijah?" That is the cry of many today facing difficult situations and stormy seasons in their lives.

Don't Just Break Through, BREAK FREE! Teaches and edifies, with each chapter referenced by the Holy Bible. This cleverly written piece speaks of the faithfulness of God's heart; ever so reminding us that in the midst of the storm He says, "I will never leave you nor forsake you" (Hebrews 13:5). So many people are burdened by the demands of day-to-day life: heavy workloads, providing for family, paying bills, and busyness in general, that they reference God only as an after thought. Off you go making plans, setting goals and securing your 401K. You have your hands in *this* venture and *that* pursuit…trying to fulfill *your* American Dream! So with your life map in hand, you chart your course and take off–full speed ahead–towards a man-made destination. Meanwhile...God may be gently nudging you in another direction.

Only if you can learn how to slow down, roll down the windows of your life, feel the breeze on your face, and enjoy the scenery along the way! There's going to be detours, forks in the road, and roadblocks on the road to spiritual freedom. But beloved, you must readjust the rear-view mirror of your past and let God direct your focus ahead! You must look at set backs as mere delays, and not ultimate defeats; pain and disappointment as character builders; and testing and trials as faith strengtheners, not dream crushers! Only then will you be able to periodically stop along the way, bask in *The Son* (Jesus), and refill your tank for the rest of this journey! God reroutes our course according to *His* plan. The sooner you accept His will for your life, the sooner you will get to your destination at Godspeed! Amen!

Don't Just Break Through, BREAK FREE! allows you to stop from time to time, get a dose of inspiration, renew your faith, share a laugh, and reflect on God's goodness! It has pearls of wisdom everyone can enjoy, from those who don't know God to seasoned Christians alike: moms, teachers, professionals, artists, dads, grandmothers, on down to teens and tweens. Warning! In order to fully grasp this book you must have a child like spirit and a hearty sense of humor! This book is not a straightforward read, per se, but offers bits and pieces of uplifting *"Mood busters"* to brighten any gloomy day! But most importantly, I believe it speaks directly to the spirit–using empirical knowledge–to instill hope, renew your faith, and remind you that God has never left nor forsaken you!

This book helps you to get back on your spiritual road to believing: Believing in yourself again, believing in your calling, and most importantly; believing that God does have a plan for your life! The Bible says with man it is impossible, but with God all things are possible! *(Matthew 19:26).*

Join thousands of other Christians who have **BROKEN FREE** from spiritual barriers by utilizing the valuable teaching in this book, and are enjoying happy, joy-filled lives and deliverance from bondage!

Don't Just Break Through,
BREAK FREE!

FREE

FREE

He knocked and the door was opened

There I stood, frozen, in the presence of Serenity

He smiled on me

All of my sins were purged

He hath set me free

The scars of this world I bear no more

Enlightened is my mind

Dead is my body

Free is my soul

Uplifted to an ethereal plane

Pale white

Pearly gates

No hostility in the air

Beauty

Peace

Tranquility

Stood up there!

A bright beam shined on me,

Then I awoke

Behold, I stand at the door and knock. If anyone hears My voice and opens the door, I will come in to him and dine with him, and he with me. Revelation 3:20.

THANK YOU!

For those who said I wasn't good enough, thank you! It caused me to shift gears into overdrive and work extra hard to fulfill my dreams.

For those who said I thought I was too good, thank you! It caused me to look within and appreciate the person God created me to be and, it showed me that I am a diligent student, striving to model my life based on the principles of the word of God.

For those who said I wasn't smart enough, thank you! It caused me to be the professor of my own classroom and self-educate myself to fill in the gaps where the educational system often fails inner city youth. Thank you for the books that took me on a journey all around the world in my mind!

Thank you to those who said I wasn't pretty enough! It taught me that beauty is a compassionate heart, loving spirit, integrity, honesty, and human kindness. Thank you! It allowed God to plant the fruits of the spirit within me (Galatians 5:22-24), which I am happy to see are sprouting daily!

For those who said I was too fat (or too skinny), thank you! It propelled me on the road to health and fitness. It caused me to take charge of my own health, and not be another statistic to diabetes, high blood pressure, cancer, and sickness.

Thank you to those who wouldn't hire me. It taught me how to trust and wait on the Lord for the job that He has for me. It caused me to know that the steps of a righteous man are ordered by the Lord: ***"The heart of man plans his way, but*** *the Lord establishes his steps" (Proverbs 16:9 ESV).*

Thank you to those who fired me, it caused me to take control of my own destiny and not depend on man for my future! It taught me that God closed those doors to steer me on the path to my appointed calling.

Thank you for not loving me because it forced me to find the courage to love myself! I now know that *I AM* worthy, *I AM* valuable, *I AM* loveable, *I AM* precious. I am the apple of God's eye! *(Zechariah 2:8)*. It taught me that where my own love fails, God's love is Perfect.

For those who walked out of my life, thank you! It opened the door for great people to enter! Thank you for teaching me that people come into our lives for a reason, a season and an appointed time. Thank you! It taught me that I was either the teacher or the student at that time in my life; either way, I learned valuable lessons.

For those who lied on me, thank you! Jesus gives me comfort in knowing that in spite of, I am blessed anyway *(Matthew 5:10-12)*. He gives me the strength to smile through my pain.

While your lies spread like a virus, I patiently waited on the Lord because He said: ***"But they who wait for the Lord shall renew their strength; they shall mount up with wings like eagles; they shall run and not be weary; they shall walk and not faint" (Isaiah 40:31 ESV).*** I'm still standing.

For those who ostracized me, thank you! It drove me down on my knees to God in prayer, and He told me that I am: ***"A chosen generation, a royal priesthood, a holy nation, His own special people, that you may proclaim the praises of Him who called you out of darkness into his marvelous light" (1 Peter 2:9).***

Thank you! It caused me to sympathize with the dejected, outcasts, and the rejects of this world. Furthermore, I contend to follow Moses' example: ***"Choosing rather to be mistreated with the people of God than to enjoy the fleeting pleasures of sin" (Hebrews 11:25 ESV).***

Thank you to those who rejected me! Because of you I now know that in God's sight I am chosen and precious! *(1Peter 2:4).* Your renunciation was only a minute indifference compared to the rejection of my Lord and Savior Jesus Christ: ***For He was the Chief cornerstone that the builders rejected (Acts 4:11, Psalm 118:22).***

Thank you to those who were hateful to me. For it taught me how to love others with the love of Christ. I chose to override your hate with the belief that we are all one in God: ***"And He has made from one blood every nation of men to dwell on all the face of the earth..." (Acts 17:26).***

It taught me that love gives and does not take. It frees and does not hold others in bondage.

Thank you to those who made me cry. Every time I cry, God cleanses my soul with *His* tears. He comforts me with His promise that: ***"Weeping may endure for a night, But joy*** *comes in the morning" (Psalm 30:5).*

Most importantly, I found out that God loves me so much that He puts my tears into a bottle! *(Psalm 56:8).*

Thank you to those who were insensitive to my handicaps. I tearfully asked God why am I different, ***"And He said to me, My grace is sufficient for you, for My strength is made perfect in weakness. Therefore, most gladly I will rather boast in my infirmities, that the power of Christ may rest upon me" (2 Corinthians 12:9 NKJV).*** I agree with the Apostle Paul! Thank you! It allows me to have compassion for those who are physically, mentally, or emotionally challenged. It taught me that all handicaps are not visible, and to treat others as I would like to be treated.

I extend the utmost gratitude. If it were not for you, I would have never known who I am in Christ. I would have never known that ***I am fearfully and wonderfully made! (Psalm 139:14).*** I would have never gotten on the highway to my divine destination.

Again I say, thank you!

Some of you may have experienced set backs, rejection, racism or discrimination in your life. I ask that you do not allow your past to make you bitter. Don't be the victim, be the difference! Defeat is designed to steer you in the right direction, get you out of your comfort zone, and get you to step out on faith! It is all a part of God's divine plan. You are the only one standing in your way. Defy the odds, break down walls and barriers, and proclaim your freedom!

Most importantly, build bridges for others to cross who walk in your footsteps!

PRAYER

As Christians, we fight our battles on our knees!

*

The sword your enemies use to stab you in the back is your sword in the spirit!

*

Yesterday's prayer won't due...for today has its own set of challenges.

*

Not praying over your day is a spiritual attack waiting to happen!

*

When you talk to God in prayer, do you stay long enough in His presence to hear what He has to say back to you?

*

At times when you pray it may feel cold and desolate. Just start moving your lips and the Holy Spirit will catch up with you!

*

Not only that we should hear your voice O Lord, but that we obey! *1 Samuel 15:22.*

*

Although satan is raising up a formidable army, God is raising up mighty warriors! Join the revolution– Pray!

*

When you pray you are reiterating back to God the promises He has already put in your heart. Now stand on faith to receive it!

*

Don't worry…pray! You can't worry and pray at the same time!

*

Cover your prayer time! Before you start praying, invite the Holy Spirit! Ask Him to block out all opposing voices. Ask him to seat ministering angels on your right and on your left.

*

God already gave you what you prayed for; He wants to s-t-r-e-t-c-h your faith to receive it!

*

Psst…looking for God? (In a hush tone) Try the prayer closet! Prayer changes things!

*

God hears and answers our prayers. *1 John 5:14-15.*

*

When you pray for the poor and destitute, you are sending love with God's heart and a hug with His arms. *Deuteronomy 10:18.*

*

Every time you pray for your brethren, you are healing a nation! Do we have any faith healers? *James 5:16.*

*

When you are urgently prompted by the Holy Spirit to pray, you are intervening evil unaware. *Romans 8:26.*

*

Do you really believe in your heart that God is going to give you what you pray for, or do you just pray to see what happens? Humm…Prayer Roulet? *Mark 11:24.*

*

Every time you think about it…pray about it!

For what great nation is there that has God so near to it, as the Lord our God is to us, for whatever reason we may call upon Him? Deuteronomy 4:7.

Healing Balm Cafe:
The Introduction

Greetings! Welcome to the Healing Balm Cafe; a place where you get the Good Word, laughter, truth, Christian entertainment, and maybe even a revelation or two!

My name is **AGAPE LOVE** and I'm the master of ceremonies! Our line up consists of:

JC REPPA: Rapper for Jesus Christ, a.k.a East Coast Soldier, Prophet Rapper–from that preacher/poet inside all of us.

GRANDMA GOSPEL: A.k.a Granny Gospel. From that place in our heart that is missing that "ole'" school, southern, sanctified, praying church mother.

And last but not least…

PHAT JOHNNY: From that part of our consciousness that wars against the flesh and is so mischievous, we just have to laugh at ourselves sometimes. *A.k.a* the instigator!

God *Is* Love

A reflection of Love...

A Perfect love that is everlasting: *John 3:16.*

A Prisoner of love: *Luke 22:54-6.*

Love is a battlefield!: *Luke 22:47-53.*

The cross models the perfect way we should love: first receive it vertically, and then distribute it horizontally.

God is...the love that I was trying to find in another human being!

It takes courage to love, cowardice to hate.

If we love one another, God abides in us, and His love has been perfected in us. *1 John 4:12.*

God, with your breath of life in me, help me to breathe love on your people.

God, let my heart sync with yours. Let it beat with the love of compassion, pump life into the sick, transfuse the Blood of Jesus into the dying, and resuscitate the hopeless.

Love is...1 Corinthians 13:4-8.

Love is...one Man who died so that the world can live.

When the heart's canvass is freed to love, it begins to paint life in a collage of peace, tolerance, and forgiveness.

Is your soul transparent? Can you see right through to God's heart?

A new commandment I give to you, That you love one another; as I have loved you, that you also love one another. John 13:34.

Felt Like Giving Up Lately?

Let's face it, life is not fair! There have been things that have happened in your life that were cruel, unjust, or just plain evil! You may have had people in your life along the way that hurt or mistreated you, abused you, cheated on you or left you! In life there are no guarantees—not even for Christians! You were deeply hurt by romantic relationships, friends, family, or co-workers, and questionably, there is seemingly no explanation. Moreover, to shoot a dagger into an already broken heart; it may feel like God is far away. Beloved, you are not alone! The Bible says in 1 Peter 5:9, that the same kinds of sufferings are being experienced by your brothers throughout the world. Sometimes when you go through painful or hurtful situations, you may feel like you are all alone. You wallow in self-pity and isolate yourself thinking: "No one cares about what I'm going through." You lack the strength to fight yet one more battle. And sadly, you may think that God is punishing you.

As a young Christian, I made the mistake of thinking that once I gave my life to God, I would not suffer—or suffer persecution, for that matter. Quite honestly, my life has been the exact opposite! It's like the devil got a memo: **New Christian convert, prepare to attack!** I was truly persecuted on every side. In my formative Christian years I went through a season of anger because of the suffering I endured, and also because I felt that I was not delivered from things from my past that was still causing me to suffer. At the time, I could not understand how a loving God could allow me to go through so much pain and despair. But beloved, I now know that God had a plan! God allowed me to go through all that hurt and pain to use it to share the Gospel; to create compassion in me for the lost, hurting and abused. Moreover, to be an ambassador for God's faithfulness and grace to people who see their lives in mine. Albeit, it would be years before I would grow in Christ and mature in His word. The Bible says that all who desire to live godly in Christ Jesus will suffer persecution (2 Timothy 3:12). It is important to learn that Christians will endure the same trials, hardships, suffering, and even loss as the world, but the difference is, we have a Savior who gives us peace in the midst of our heartache, calm in the midst of our despair, and is a healing balm in the midst of our pain.

Peace I leave with you, My peace I give to you; not as the world gives do I give to you. Let not your heart be troubled, neither let it be afraid (John 14:27).

Moreover, in God we have hope which the world doesn't have! God may allow many tests and trials in your life but you will not be defeated by them. All you have to do is call out to Him. At times of duress is especially when you need to cry out to God and seek Him more aggressively. But some people do the opposite: they shut down and hope the problem will go away, or try to solve the problem themselves. Some people find it hard to pray at troubling times, they may feel like their prayers aren't being answered. In the beginning of my prayer life I struggled with some of the same issues. I would try to pray to God, but often felt like my prayers were bouncing off the wall, not getting through. But I desperately wanted to know the purpose for my life and the reason I kept going through so many awful things, so I persistently kept seeking His face.

I now realize that God had to allow me to go through some of those things to perfect my prayer language. Have you ever been in so much pain that you're desperate? That situation hurt so bad, it brought you past your knees, down to the ground on your face, prostrate before God like King David in 2 Samuel 12:1, when his son died? That pain was the key that unlocked my spiritual door! God had to allow me to get to the end of myself, my lowest point, only then would I be able to surrender all. When I hit rock bottom, that's when I met God in my prayer closet, down on the floor! That's how I learned to intercede in prayer. Saints, you have to learn how to press in. Don't let your prayer life be dictated by your emotions and feelings. I thought that when I prayed I was supposed to feel God's presence in a tangible way. Whether you feel His presence or not, pray on anyhow! You have to learn to keep praying until you breakthrough to heaven.

Oftentimes people approach their relationship with God the same way they do human relationships. They expect God to relate to them in a perceptible manner. But the difference is, when you communicate with a physical human being, you have the ability to gauge body language, facial expression and emotions; then you react accordingly. But when you pray (talk) to God, it's in spirit; there is no physical body to relate to so it requires a great level of trust. Trust that God hears you, trust that what His word says is true, and trust that whatever you are going through is under His control. The devil will try to tell you that God is not listening to you. More so, he will do everything he can to try to distract you from praying or try to get you to believe that prayer doesn't work. That's why it is imperative that you make up your mind to emphatically trust God no matter what it looks like or feels like.

It also takes a certain level of persistence in prayer. Keep pressing in, pushing through until you get through to the spirit realm. Overtime you will notice your prayer life expanding into longer prayer times and you will begin to have a deeper intimacy with the Father. I am a living witness of answered prayer, pressing through, touching the heart of God! Some things that I have prayed years for, I have seen God unfold right in front of my very eyes! I cannot begin to describe the feeling when you see how God has answered your petitions. Beloved it's a simple fact that suffering is tantamount to Christianity. Whether it is a brief season of suffering or a permanent thorn in your flesh like that of the Apostle Paul. In 2 Corinthians 12:8, he states that he "pleaded with the Lord three times," that it might depart from him! You will go through peaks and valleys, and spiritual highs overshadowed by faith testing lows. I wish I could say it will be smooth sailing, but it won't.

There are just some things you must go through that only suffering will produce the kind of fruit in you needed to serve in God's kingdom. A fruit that gives you a heart of compassion, a heart for people, and a hunger for God. If we examine the Apostle Paul's life after his conversion from Saul, he was an ambassador traveling from region to region proclaiming the Gospel of Jesus Christ; but nonetheless, a messenger of satan was sent to buffet him the course of his whole Christian journey! But beloved the good news is, God says, **"My grace is sufficient for you, for My strength is made perfect in weakness" (2 Corinthians 12:7-9).** It's those thorns that keep us humbled, that doesn't let us swell up with pride and arrogance and that keeps us dependent on God.

I have learned it's mostly about your attitude when going through difficult times. Do you complain, grumble and murmur like the children of Israel in the wilderness? Sometimes people endure suffering longer than necessary by being malcontent and disgruntled. In the beginning of my Christian walk I spent too much time than I care to admit in the desert of life because of an unappreciative and unthankful attitude. Conversely, what I was beginning to see–through times of hardship–was how God was producing character, patience and faith in me. It truly was bittersweet. That's why the Bible tells us to glory in our tribulations: **And not only that, but we also glory in tribulations, knowing that tribulation produces perseverance; and perseverance, character;**

and character, hope (Romans 5:3,4).

For many years I struggled with this verse. I just could not relate it to my misery. Why would I find glory in suffering? But after meditating on it, I learned it's not that I am glad this bad thing happened to me, but I am glad because of the change in character it produced in me. You must learn to hold onto God, and allow Him to be your guiding light through the dark nights of your life. Though you may weep, have assurance that joy will come in the morning! (Psalm 30:5). Quite honestly, I believe God allowed me to go through some of the things I went through because I was too impatient. Not only was patience a character trait I needed developed, I learned not to go ahead of God. I learned to wait on His timing, His deliverance, and His solution to the problem. When you take your hands off your problems and give them to God, and learn to just rest in His peace, that's when you will begin to see how God is working things out in your life. Beloved, when you go through the fire a few times and come out unscathed, that's when you will begin to see God's hand of protection covering you, and therefore learn to trust Him in every area of your life.

The more trials you face, the more you will see God's faithfulness and mercy in your life. It gives you a deeper conviction and fervor for Christ. It gives you a greater testament to the faithfulness of God. Additionally, it gives you a closer more profound walk with God. Have you ever met someone who has really been through something? Somebody who's been to hell and back, and who God delivered out of the trenches of death? The anointing just emanates from them! It exudes the heart of God. Beloved, the book of Psalms was written out of that suffering!

When facing a difficult situation, you have to diligently remind yourself to walk by faith and not by sight (2 Corinthians 5:7). Yes, you may hear that verse time and time again, but you must reflectively incorporate it into your daily life. Oftentimes I theorize Christians as soldiers going to the battlefield. We will be gravely defeated if we aren't suited for the war. All we have to do is show up wearing our armor (Ephesians 6:10-18), but it is God who will fight our battles! (2 Chronicles 20:15). You cannot be complacent in the Kingdom of God. You simply cannot just do nothing. Being a Christian involves constant change; evolving, growing, maturing. You have to prepare yourself in advance of attacks, and in the midst of an attack saturate yourself in the presence of God. The following are tools for spiritual warfare that will help you when you are faced with difficult situations:

1. Read the Bible: Look up scriptures that pertain to your situation. It will not only take your mind off the problem, but you will be actively committing scripture to memory.

2. Pray without ceasing: When you are going through a trial don't just rely on others to pray for you,

you can get through to God as well! You *must* be proactive in your own Prayer life.

3. Read Christian books: Arm yourself with books by authors who have gone through what you may be going through to find out how they overcame the situation. Besides the Bible, we should carry Christian books with us at all times. I cannot tell you how many times I've been encouraged and uplifted just from reading other people's testimony in the midst of a bad day.

4. Praise and worship music: Beloved, God ministers through music! There has been many times God has ministered to my heart through song. There's a sweet peace that resonates in Christian music. More, there will be some times you'll find it hard to pray. Some praise/worship music is prayer in song!

5. Podcasts/Youtube: I love, love podcasts and youtube! You can literally go to church right in the middle of your living room! At a click of the mouse, you can get a word for any situation you are going through! Sometimes social media can be a great study partner!

6. Internet search: With advanced technology, Christians today have it so much easier that there is just no excuse not to study God's word. Just do a search on any topic for online inspiration.

7. Call and pray for/with somebody else: Aiding others helps your problems seem nominal! The Bible also says give and it will be given to you, the same measure you use will be measured back to you! (Luke 6:38).

Don't take defeat lying down! As soon as an attack comes, arm yourself with your spiritual weapons and drown out the enemy's voice. Over the years, I've learned to relinquish my control to the prayer closet instead of trying to fix my problems with debating, confrontation or arguing. There will be days when life seems too hard to bear. Those are the times our Father is calling us closer to Him: to cast out, bind, *plead the Blood* on His behalf. Oftentimes, that is what it takes to get us out of complacency; to get us to be proactive instead of reactive.

Unbeknownst to us, there are things conspiring in the spirit realm that our physical eyes just cannot see and mind cannot comprehend. If God only gave you a glimpse into the spirit world you would be terrified beyond measure. That's why you must cover yourself with prayer! And lastly, how will you truly know that God is a provider, redeemer, and healer if you never went through anything to see how He has delivered you out? It should be your prayer that God would allow any fiery darts from the enemy that are meant to refine and perfect you. When you feel like Gideon going into battle against the behemoth army of the Midianites, just know that God is working it out behind the scenes according to His plan...but for your glory!

I have been young, and now am old; Yet I have not seen the righteous forsaken, Nor his descendants begging bread (Ps. 37:25).

An Evening At
The Healing Balm Cafe

AGAPE LOVE: Welcome back to the Healing Balm Cafe! It's a pleasure to have you join us this evening! I'm *Agape Love* and I will be your master of ceremonies! We have a spectacular line up tonight—so check your problems at the door, hang up your coat of despair, and revive your spirit with a hot cup of soul caffeine! Enjoy the show!

AGAPE LOVE: First up to the mic, please help me welcome *JC Reppa,* a.k.a Jesus Christ Representer, a.k.a East Coast Soldier, a.k.a The Prophet Rapper to the stage...

JC REPPA: (Raps) He's hot on my tail like the FBI, tryna entice, seduce...catch me up in a crime. Satan, you can't stop my flow, you tryna creep in through da back doe, 'cause of His SON...I'm already out the window...ahead ah ya mane...

GRANDMA GOSPEL: (Interrupting rap) BOY YOU BETTA TELL IT!...Oh...I almost lost my teef!

JC REPPA: (Angry about interruption...continues) My God has already been arrested, hung and crucified—so satan I'M FREE ON A HEAVENLY BOND! Yeaaah son!...

*The dialect of these characters are written phonetically to capture the true essence of Southern and urban street slang.

GRANDMA GOSPEL: (Screaming) BACK IN DA DAY WE USED TA...lemme come up there on dat stage...(goes up on the stage and grabs mic).

GRANDMA GOSPEL: (Still screaming into mic) BACK IN MY DAY...

PHAT JOHNNY: Granny deaf gums (screams), YOU DON'T HAVE TO SCREAM!!!

GRANDMA GOSPEL: DAT'S GRANNY GOSPEL TO YOU! (Rolls eyes and lowers tone) Like I wuz sayin'...we used ta sang dose ole' gospel hymns like: (Starts singing) *'Goin' up aah y-o-n-d-e-e-r...to be with my Laaawd'* (voice cracks)...

PHAT JOHNNY:
Holyghostfilledsanctifiedandshootin' the guns of the spirit...we don't wanna hear dat!

PHAT JOHNNY: This is a new era, we up on some Kanye West!

GRANNY GOSPEL: Oh he did sing *Jesus Walks*.

PHAT JOHNNY: You so old...it looks like you've been walking with Jesus all the way from Bethlehem!

Grandma Gospel, Phat Johnny, and JC Reppa all start arguing...*Jesus take the wheel* starts playing in the background.

AGAPE LOVE: Ladies and gentlemen, thanks for stopping by the Healing Balm Cafe. May you continue to love, laugh, and let Christ be the center of your life! Come back and visit soon!

God,
If You Are Real...

When I hear testimonies from people giving account of their lives before they became Christians, I sympathize as they recall in heart wrenching detail, choices they made that spiraled them down a road of emptiness and despair; choices, ironically, that would eventually lead them to give their lives to Christ. One day while listening to testimonies at church, I noticed a common theme: the speakers all had different stories, but the same burning request: that God prove His existence. **"God, if you are real..."** would be the proverbial sentence uttered in despair at the climax of each person's story. Beloved, out of sheer desperation or anger, many people are demanding God to answer that same call today! School and public shootings, racial profiling, xenophobia, bombings, and terrorist attacks are modern day's pressing dilemmas. As these tragedies broadcast on news stations and media outlets around the world, many are wondering why God isn't intervening. Some verbally voice sentiments of anger, and question God's existence; others question His love, deeming Him unfair and unjust. Sadly, these are *some* of the same people that pass laws to eradicate God and His likeness in the workplace, school system, sporting events, and public places; as well as reject Him in their personal lives.

Many people blame God for the world's crisis, their personal problems, and sin. But at the root of the blame is an imbalanced relationship with God, which stems from, quite simply, an aversion to God's written word. Most people refuse to obey the Bible because they want to live according to their own lusts and desires. In which they are saying, "My needs come before God's," delegating *them* God over their lives. Additionally, I have had many conversations with people–

some claiming to love God–that have said to me that the Bible is simply *impossible* to live by; further stating its rules and demands are too stringent and not attainable. More, many opine that the Bible is antiquated and not written by God; but by man, as an excuse to live lascivious lives. However, when disaster strikes, an accusatory finger is pointed at Christ by the rebellious to further prove to *themselves* that God is not real or either not righteous. So why would God intervene when so many have told Him that they do not regard His word, nor Him? Deuteronomy 31:18 says, "And I will surely hide my face in that day because of all the evil which they have done, in that they have turned to other gods." Many are leading souls astray proclaiming that Jesus Christ is not the true Savior, or stating that there is more than one road to God or heaven. Some religious doctrines teach that man is good and righteous within himself, and that by simply reciting or chanting religious verbiage, or practicing religious laws or rituals will lead them to salvation. That is a lie from hell! John 14:6 says," **I am the way, the truth, and the life. No one comes to the Father except through Me."** What I have noticed is that people who shun Christianity often favor religions that have no requirements or commitments to moral responsibility; religions that do not hold them accountable for their behavior or actions, but sadly delegates *them* god over their lives.

Joshua 24:15

And if it is evil in your eyes to serve the lord, choose this day whom you will serve, whether the gods your fathers served in the region beyond the river, or the god's of the

Amorites in whose land you dwell. But as for me and my house, we will serve the Lord."

Here in this passage Joshua is admonishing the Israelites to make a choice between serving other gods or the one true and living God! God gives us volition; in other words, the free will to *choose* to serve Him! You can't have it both ways; you have to decide either to serve God with a whole heart and fully trust Him with your life; or not serve Him at all, thus relinquishing you from blaming God for choices made outside of His will. Joshua goes on to tell the Israelites not to depend on the confidence of their flesh, but to look back over their many trials and see how God has kept them and protected them through the perils of the desert.

Herein lies the problem, many say they love God, but their love for Him is based on conditions: "What can God do for me? How can God bless me? If God prospers me, then I'll serve Him!" What's worse, their lifestyles do not line up with that of persons who are obedient to the laws of Christ. In Revelation 3:16, God says of these type of people, **"So, because you are lukewarm, and neither hot nor cold, I will spit you out of my mouth."** Being a Christian requires a *total* commitment to God and His word; it requires letting God lead your life daily, and being faithful to Him.

People love their pets. To some folks, their pets are their family. Pet owners develop a strong bond with their dogs or cats because these animals love you unconditionally. When you leave, your dog is sad to see you go; oftentimes following behind you with its head hung low, like a sad puppy (pun intended); conversely, when you return home–with tail wagging anticipation—it runs to greet you at the door. How many people wish they could get that kind of salutation from their spouse when they return home from work? Furthermore, pets don't hold grudges and are never angry with you. Animals offer emotional support, and to some, life dependent physical support. Man's best friend (hence the term) almost always cheers you up when you are not feeling your best. It is a constant companion. And the best part, its only requirement is your requited love! Now, just think about it...if you weren't faithful or committed to your pet—you didn't feed or bath it, didn't spend time with or talk to it, didn't take it out for walks or out to relieve itself—your pet would feel ignored, lonely, and unloved. Moreover, your house would be a stinkin' mess! Beloved, I believe God's love for us is just like that little dog. He wants to dote on you, love you and spend time with you, but when you ignore Him, God is heartbroken over you just as that abandoned pup! Introspectively, when you neglect God, your spiritual house is a stinkin' mess! You are driven by selfishness, pride and **Easing God Out**.

God, Where Are You?

One day a brother from my church asked if he could speak to me about something. He said that he was really burdened and that he needed someone to talk to. He explained to me that he was born with a learning disability because his mother was using drugs when she was pregnant with him. He explained to me that this made his life extremely difficult because people often ostracized, bullied, and treated him badly. He also shared that he was not competent enough to get or keep a job. He said that he felt as if he were an outcast to society, which caused him to spend a lot of time alone and isolated from others. He further elaborated that because of loneliness, he became addicted to pornography. He went on to say that he was on a roller coaster ride of addiction and wanted to be permanently set free. Desperately, he explained, he kept praying and asking God to deliver him, and it would seem to work momentarily, but after awhile he would delve right back into this gripping sin.

I sensed that he had resentment towards God, not only for his birth condition, but also because he felt that God did not deliver him from pornography, among other things he was struggling with. Although he has been going to church for over 10 years, he said that he just could not get set free from this dark part of his life. I felt led to ask him a few questions: ***How did you become a Christian? What do you do when you're not in church? Where do you spend most of your time? And, who do you spend your time with?*** He replied that his mother is a Christian and through her prompting he started going to church. Additionally, he explained that he goes to church mostly to try to meet people. He said the few friends that he does have are not Christians; further elaborating that these friends frequent places that sell pornography, and encourage his participation. Worst, he said that despite praying for years, he feels like there is no hope for him and he just feels like giving up!

What about you? Perhaps you are struggling with a sin that you just cannot seem to get delivered from; maybe you were born with a handicap, a debilitating illness or a disability; maybe you are struggling with hatred or unforgiveness because you were deeply hurt by someone you trusted. Or, maybe you were a victim of physical or sexual abuse. Perhaps you lost a loved one, went through a divorce, failed at a business/career or lost everything that was of value to you (the list can go on and on). Have you turned your back on God because you feel like He has not healed or delivered you? What's more, maybe you are *still* waiting on God to answer a prayer, or maybe you prayed for something and the end result was not what you believed God for. You too may be incredulous of faith and trust in God. You too may be asking, "God where are you?"

My friend knew about God, but he did not know God! The Bible says in James 4:8, **"Draw near to God and He will draw near to you."** The first step is getting to know God for yourself. It requires seeking a personal relationship with Christ. Some who were raised in a Christian family or taught the gospel by the pastor of their local church, falsely believe that they can inherit eternal salvation through others. Isaiah 29:13, sorrowfully states "...their fear towards Me is taught by the commandment of men." I remember as a child, my Godmother used to take me to church, and the preacher would preach so passionately about salvation. I was scared to sin just by hearing his voice! He preached with fire and brimstone! This well intended man of God taught that if a person committed a sin, they were going straight to hell! As a young child, this frightened me severely. Growing up, I felt so guilty when I sinned that I was tormented with agony that God would punish me. I had a *man made* fear of God! I thought God was just this strict authoritarian in Heaven, bestowing wrath on everyone that didn't live a perfect life. Then I met Jesus! I have since learned that *that* fear was impressed upon me by an over zealous preacher. Philippians 2:12 states, "Each man has to work out *his own* salvation." Each man has to learn the character of God, heart of God, and voice of God for himself. On my Christian journey, I would later come to know God in spirit and in truth. I also learned that God was not this angry disciplinarian, but a patient, loving, and faithful God; a God who is my friend and who convicts me when I sin. Beloved, the only thing that will sustain you in the winters of Christianity is to truly know Christ for yourself! You don't have to have it all together before you come to God, He will help you get it together! Start by simply talking to God as you would a dear friend or relative. Ask God to reveal Himself to you in a real way. It may not happen overnight, but slowly God will start to tug at your heart. You'll begin to feel a yearning for the things of God. Worldly pleasures will not appeal to you as much anymore, and you will desire to spend more time in God's presence.

    Surely with natural reasoning, you cannot understand why God created you the way that He did, but one thing is for sure: if you are a child of the Most High, you were born for His divine purpose! Furthermore, Romans 9:20, asks who are you to ask God (The Potter), "Why have you made me like this?" Sadly, many see themselves through a distorted lens: damaged, shattered, and broken; but when God looks at you, He sees a reflection of Himself–His perfect creation! The Bible says we were made in His image (Genesis 1:27), more so, Colossians 2:15, says that His Son, Christ, *is* the image of the invisible God. Therefore, if we were made in God's image, then we know that the same sufferings we are experiencing today, so did His Son Jesus Christ. Thus, verifying that Christ identifies with our weaknesses! Jesus, having been sent down to earth in human form, was rejected by man, persecuted, and too questioned the Father. But God still saw Him as precious in His sight! In the Book of John, after Jesus' baptism, the Bible says that heaven opened up, and the spirit of God descended like a dove, and spoke: **"This is my son, whom I love; with Him I am well pleased."** So therefore beloved, if God sacrificed His only son, who was at times weak in His flesh as we are, and whose *purpose* was to die on the cross for you and me, how much more does God love you and has a plan for your life! Therefore, you must learn how God feels about you. How do you do that? By researching scripture that speaks of God's love, grace, and faithfulness. Most importantly, you must *believe* what God says about you as opposed to what the world thinks about you. That is the only way you will ever have an accurate and correct view of yourself. 1 Peter 2:4, says you will be rejected by men, but are chosen by God and precious to Him. His words regarding you has to become so ingrained in your mind and spirit, that it overrules any contrary thoughts or voice from any other source.

In conclusion, Christ was persecuted, ostracized, rejected, and He suffered; and at the completion of His assignment on earth, He was killed. God then exalted Him to heaven. Though in this body, earth is not our home. We will suffer because, as Christians, we are not of this world. Our eternal home is in Heaven. When this life of striving is over, God will exalt us to the highest place: His Kingdom, where there will be no more suffering, no more pain, no more weeping (Revelation 21:4). When you went up to the altar and first gave your life to God, it may have been an euphoric feeling, but you can't just live off of that one moment of joy and go back living your life the way you used to. The altar is where you lay down your life and pick up your cross! As stated in the last chapter, a lot of Christians base their relationship with God according to their emotions. Many think that they should always be able to *feel* God's presence, and know His direction all the time. That is simply not true. Sometimes God will be silent, or allow you to go a roundabout way, like the children of Israel, because you are not yet spiritually matured for the job He has called you to do. Or worst, because of disobedience. When you surrender your life to God, you are called to live by faith, not feelings.

Beloved, you must make the word come alive in your life! You must put it into practice daily, you must listen to and abide by it. You are not going to become a powerful Christian by *just* listening to a sermon or Bible reading. Yes, you should read your Bible, but simply reading or hearing the word only, and not *doing* your part and further educating yourself–even if you have a mountain hill of faith–won't give you the tools needed to defeat the enemies of your soul. Many people neglect the disciplines of the Gospel, but *expect* God to do all the spiritual work for them! The Bible says, "Faith by itself, if it does not have works, is dead" (James 2:17). Moreover, a lot of people keep God on the back burner of their lives, and when problems and disasters arise, expect God to be a magic genie and immediately fix all their woes. It doesn't work like that. You must work on your Christian life daily and God will respond to your to your obedience!

Lesson: you cannot expect to be a devil-defeating, test-enduring, persevering Christian and not do the required spiritual work: praying, reading your Bible, studying, fasting, prophesying over your life and going to church.

If you do not adhere to these principles, you will always fold under pressure! Being a successful Christian requires making sacrifices for God, and living a disciplined life. In no way am I saying that the aforementioned guarantees total deliverance from all of your problems, but beloved, what I am saying is that when you make a habit of doing these things, you are planting seeds into the soil of your spirit; allowing God to grow and strengthen your inner man. Therefore, when problems do arise, you will be better equipped to handle them. God will do the plowing, pulling out of the weeds, killing of spiritual bugs, and ultimately fertilize your growth in Him. 1 Corinthians 3:6 says, "I planted, Apollos watered, but God gave the growth." I love this verse because it takes the burden and fear away from me of trying to fix myself, or change in my own strength. All I have to do is keep planting spiritual seeds by being diligent in my Christian walk, and God will grow my thinking, wisdom and knowledge in Him!

To be a powerful, persevering Christian that is able to run this race with endurance, tenacity and longevity, there are four areas you must conquer: **disciplining your mind, being holy, trusting God, and repentance.**

__Disciplining the mind__

The Bible says, "Let this mind be in you that is in Christ" (Philippians 2:5). When you convert to Christianity, disciplining your mind is the first area you must focus on. Although you have given your life to God, your mind is still attuned to the thinking of the world; its views regarding success, money, relationships, happiness and even your self-image. When you become a Christian, your focus should shift to God's perception of these areas for your life. When you neglect to do the spiritual work, you will say that you are a Christian, but your behavior and lifestyle will be no different than that of your non-Christian counterparts. That's why the Bible strongly admonishes us to come out from among them (the world), and be separate (2 Corinthians 6:17). Some foolishly think that they can receive the blessings of God and live compromising lives and worship the idols of this world.

Moreover, there will be mental strongholds and pre-programmed thinking embedded in your mind by your family, the environment you grew up in, media, and political or social circles you're in that you may have thought were normal. Until you diligently study God's word to align your mind with the Bible's point of view, you may not be aware of the adulterated way you think or react to people and situations. On this Christian journey, I have been humbled to my knees in prayer many times after eye-opening situations where God mercifully revealed to me what was in my heart. Beloved, many of these things you may not even know are deeply hidden until God allows a difficult circumstance or trial to bring it to surface. Many sins of the heart include: jealousy, insecurity, pride, vengeance, self-righteousness, and unforgiveness–just to name a few.

The devil is working overtime to destroy families, relationships, communities and society as a whole, by targeting the mind with false perceptions and expectations. How? Through pop culture, television, music, radio, mass media, even educational institutions. He is starting as early as toddlers, implanting subliminal or provocative messages through seemingly innocuous avenues such as cartoons, toys, and even their schools. The devil's creating a facade of what true happiness is by manipulating the minds of vulnerable men, women, children through false advertising that says a person has to look a certain way, attain a certain income or social status, or marry a certain type of mate in order to be successful. Many are falling victim to this worldly agenda by measuring themselves and their self-worth against the images presented to them through this subliminal marketing scheme, and not surprisingly, they are finding that they don't measure up! Hence, they develop a *wrong* self-image of themselves, and often become depressed, bitter, and angry; subjectively feeling like failures. Rightfully so! 2 Corinthians 5:17, gives the body of Christ a spiritual mirror to gauge their self-worth. It states, **"Therefore, if any man be in Christ, he is a new creation; old things are passed away; behold all things are become new."** This verse is saying that as Christians we have been renewed, therefore we are no longer subject to who or what the world says we are, but our identity is in Christ! We must learn to see our reflection in the Bible, and not in the world.

Because of the pressure to measure up to society's standards, the devil is tormenting many people with spirits of **fear, worry, anxiety, defeat,** and **failure.** According to the **National Center For Health Statistics (NCHS)**, as of this writing, 11% of Americans aged 12 and older are on some form of anti-depressant. There is a war that is being waged against the mind by a formidable, ominous opponent–the devil. Millions are becoming increasingly addicted to prescription drugs, narcotics, synthetic drugs, marijuana, or alcohol hoping a pill or liquor will make all of their problems go away. Don't get me wrong, there are people suffering from serious medical conditions that only a trained physician can cure through medication; but what I am talking about is the many cases where people have become dependent on drugs, trying to anesthetize their spiritual pain.

Many are struggling with depression, emotional problems, negative thinking, self-harming, eating disorders, self-hatred and sleeping problems. They feel that this is just the way they are and that there is no way out, or help for them. For some, it is a battle just to get out of bed every morning to face the day. I know this first hand because this was once me. I remember one day, a loved one got so tired of my self-loathing and feeling sorry for myself, she told me,**"Look, you don't have to live like this! Change your thinking and change your life!"** Those words echoed throughout the crevices of my soul. They stayed with me. I thought depression was my lot in life, I thought this was just the way God made me. She said, "No, you can change!"

I thank God for putting that voice of reason in my life! Thus, I began the journey of self-healing! My first step was researching and finding books on what I was going through. I started educating myself and studying about the mind. I learned how to challenge my thoughts and not accept every thought that popped into my mind. I learned how to shift my thoughts from negative thinking to applying hope to every problem in my life. Most importantly, I learned the importance of reciting positive affirmations everyday until my thinking automatically shifted to optimism instead of pessimism! Maybe you are at this point in your life right now. Don't let your thoughts defeat you anymore! You have a choice to think another thought and replace it with the truth. Line every thought up with the word of God. If a thought is contrary to what the Bible espouses–love, peace and harmony–you know it is not from God! If a thought pops into my mind that goes against God's word, then I know that thought is from the devil, or my own human rationing. Saints, that's why it is so important to read the Bible everyday because the enemy's implanted thoughts are sometimes so subtle, many times you will not even be aware that you are even thinking them. The word of God exposes and uproots wrong thoughts–it brings them to light.

In continuation, did you know that the Bible says that unbelief is a sin? (John 16:9). Sadly, a lot of people are blood washed, Holy-Ghost filled saints, but are greatly defeated in this area! I was one of them! For years I would wonder why I would go to church, come back home filled with the Spirit, and the next day I'm depressed, knocked down and defeated. It's because my mind was not *disciplined*. No one told me I had to study in the area of the mind! I thought once I got saved, everything I was struggling with would automatically take care of itself. No! I had to put in the work! At a point in my life when it seemed like everything was falling apart, I became very hungry for God's word. That led me to start taking notes at church, going home and doing my own

Biblical research, and studying throughout the week! Many church goers succumb to spiritual attacks and are defeated in their daily walk because they are starved of the Word! You cannot eat a good, satisfying meal on Sunday and expect it to last you throughout the whole week! You have to eat from the Word of God everyday!

The Bible says,

"Man shall not live by bread alone, but man lives by every word that proceeds from the mouth of the Lord" (Deuteronomy 8:3).

In summation, the number one way the devil attacks you is through your mind. The second most efficient way the enemy attacks you is through people. Think about it. We live with people in our homes, we work with people at our the jobs, when we travel, shop, run errands...yup! People are there! Outside of yourselves, it is simply the most effective way for satan to attack you. There is no way to get around it–unless however, you live in a cave! If you don't spend time with God before you leave the house, you are a spiritual train wreck waiting to derail! Most importantly, if you don't discipline your mind, you will not be skilled in recognizing the tactics the enemy uses to undermine your self-worth and your relationships: you will take things personally, be vengeful, combative, easily offended, think wrongly of people, make false assumptions, or assume things that are not there. After many regretful, embarrassing and humbling situations, God began to show me the caliber of my thoughts–which originate from the heart. After years of wrestling in this area I started reciting this prayer:

Psalms 51:10

Create in me a clean heart, O God, And renew a steadfast spirit within me.

I like to say this prayer because essentially I am asking God to keep reminding me and showing me things that have crept into my spirit that I do not notice are there. Find a prayer dealing with your particular problem and recite it daily; ask God to constantly remind you when you have allowed uncleanliness to enter your heart.

Beloved, in order to gain victory over your mind, dodge arrows the devil shoots at you, and turn fear into fearlessness, you have to become proactive in getting your mind spiritually in shape to be able to endure the challenges you will face as a Christian. 2 Corinthians 10:4, tells us that: **"Though we walk in the flesh, we do not war according to the flesh."** Your mind is where the devil will strongly attack you. If he can attack your mind, every area of your life will be defeated! Think of your mind as a car's engine. The engine it what gives a car its life. If the engine does not work, the car won't start, the lights won't turn on, the tires won't rotate. It may look good on the outside, but internally it does not function properly! So is the mind; if your thinking is faulty not only will you be crippled in your relationship with yourself, but also your family, romantic, and professional relationships.

Being Holy

Tell me where you spend your time and money, and I'll tell you where your heart is! If you begin to take inventory of your day-to-day routine, you will slowly begin to see what takes priority in your life. Some things may not be considered bad, but may steal precious time, or take dominance over things that you could be doing that will help you learn, grow, and be more productive; things like spending countless hours watching TV, playing video games or shopping. Contrarily, there are other things people engage in that are destroying their families, finances, careers, and health. Destructively, it has gotten such a tight grip on them that they feel like they have no control over it. Maybe you know of someone who is having an affair, addicted to drugs or alcohol, is a gambler, or addicted to pornography. It may be you! Certainly your life's dream was not to be this thing. But somehow, you left a door open to sin, and this temptation has moved into your spirit and made a home. This is the cry of many voices in the wilderness. **"It was innocent fun, flirtation, passing time, and it turned into this,"** many, many say who are struggling with a transgression. Sadly, some are so deep in their sin they do not want to turn away from it, even though it is killing them! That's why it is very important to guard what you allow into your spirit. Those things you innocently entertain, things you may assume are harmless are the very things fighting God for your soul!

The five senses are gateways to the spirit realm:

Eyes

A lot of programming in today's media is laden with profanity, fornication, immorality, and self-gratification. If you continue to allow yourself to absorb such content, over time your mind begins to send subconscious messages to your spirit that lewd acts, aberrant activity, unnatural behavior, and foul-language are acceptable; the norm. Moreover, explicit TV programs, pornographic movies, strip clubs, X-rated magazines and the like, *entice* people to sin and oftentimes create a desire to carry out theses acts.

Ears

As a child of God, be very careful who and what you listen to. If a person's advice isn't Biblically based, they may give you a wrong view, or lead you in the wrong direction. If you entertain people who are negative and morose they will drain you emotionally and spiritually; also you may start to acquire their outlook on life. More, music that dishonors God, music that is misogynistic or immoral, philosophical rhetoric that devalues Christianity, class lectures that conditions you to the world's way of thinking, and New Age schools of thought, can desensitize you to the truth found in Jesus Christ. These are all carefully constructed tools authored by satan to dismantle God's Word. One must be very vigilant in guarding his spirit from the world's propaganda.

Touch

In 2 Corinthians 6:17, the Lord admonishes us to separate ourselves from uncleanliness and perversion. He commands us to, **"Touch no unclean thing, and I will receive you!"** Joshua chapter 6, tells of the story of the Jericho wall falling down. God commanded Joshua to go march around the city of Jericho seven days and He will give it and its kings over to him. So Joshua obeyed the Lord and marched around the wall seven times along with the priests carrying the Ark of the Covenant of the Lord, and on the seventh day the Bible says," **So the people shouted when the priests blew with the trumpets: and it came to pass, when the people heard the sound of the trumpet, and the people shouted with a great shout, that the wall fell down flat, so that the people went into the city, every man straight before him and they took the city."** Before they sieged Jericho, God sternly warned the Israelites in Joshua 6:18, not to take *any* cursed items from Jericho. **"And you, by all means abstain from the accursed things, lest you become accursed when you take of the accursed things."** He went on to say if they did take forbidden items they will curse their own land and trouble it! When you read pornography magazines, place statues of idols in your house, have an affair with (touch) another person's spouse, you are indeed cursing your own life!

Mouth/Nose

The mouth can be used to bless, but also to curse. Besides eating, some use it as nothing more than an exit point for foul language, belittling, anger, and gossip. A Christian must learn to guard his or her mouth. James 1:26 says, **"If anyone thinks he is religious and does not bridle his tongue but deceives his heart, this person's religion is worthless " (ESV). James 3:5 says, "Even so the tongue is a little member and boasts great things. See how great a forest a little fire kindles!" Verse 6 goes on to say, "The tongue is so set among our members that it defiles the whole body, and sets on fire the course of nature; and it is set on fire by hell."** You must practice using the mouth to edify, encourage and bless, not only yourself, but others! Try to be mindful of how you use your words, and think before you speak. How many times have you spoken prematurely or out of anger and wished you could take it back? People who are very judgmental and condescending destroy relationships because of a refusal to monitor their language. Make today the day you change how you communicate! Moreover, both the nose and mouth are entry points for drug use. Hanging out with the wrong crowd, trying to fit in, partying, drinking, and smoking often lead to drug use and crippling drug addiction. If you are running in those circles, ultimately someone will tell you to, "Try this, it'll make you feel better" or, give you something and persuade you that, "This will help you to relax." And unfortunately, many times *that* someone is not just the street drug dealer, but also a medical doctor! A board certified physician! Many unsuspecting people become addicted to prescription drugs prescribed by impetuous doctors. If you experience a health problem that causes you to seek medical attention, don't just take one doctor's advice concerning your problem. Get a second and third opinion if you have to! And by all means DO YOUR OWN RESEARCH! Many times there are naturopathic options to treat your problem, or another doctor may be able to avoid prescription medication all together! There was a time when I had to have major surgery. I had tumors that were growing at an accelerated rate. The first doctor I went to told me I would have to go on a very powerful drug. In my spirit it just did not feel right. I went home and did my research and, lo and behold!–there was an ongoing lawsuit against that very medication! This particular drug was so bad that many people complained of extreme side effects including: bone loss, hair loss, permanent disability, and an unfortunate few lost their life because of taking it! Beloved, we are living in a time where we not only have to be spiritually attuned, but wise! The Bible tells us to, **"See that ye walk circumspectly, not as fools, but as wise..." (Ephesians 5:15-20).** Many who are addicted to drugs will tell you all it took was *one time*, and they were hooked for life! Moreover, what many people don't realize is, there is a spirit that is operating behind the scenes that is trying to entrap your soul into eternal damnation! That spirit is satan! Not at all am I saying all media/entertainment/music is evil, but one indication that you should not be entertaining it is if you feel violated while engaging in it, if you feel convicted in your spirit, and most importantly, if it goes against the word of God! Don't even take a chance and dance with the devil! Your soul depends on it!

As Christians, God admonishes us in 1 Peter 1:16 to, **"Be ye holy; for I am holy."** Holiness does not come over night. It is a process, most, a commitment to God. Even though you decided to give your life to Christ, your mindset will still be of the world! The way you think about things and react to situations will need to be scrutinized, and that will take much time and patience. That's why I place such a strong emphasis on being diligent and proactive in your Christian walk. You *must* be studious as a Christian. It will take studying and learning God's principles to challenge those old attitudes and worldly ways of thinking. It will be by far one of the hardest, yet best things you will do after conversion. But it is well worth it once you begin to experience the peace and joy you will have in Christ!

If the spirit is not disciplined, you will not have the strength to turn off programming that devalues you, turn down that offer to get high, or suffer being alone rather than hang out with friends who are leading you down a path of destruction. You will not have the willpower to overcome lust, stop binge eating or stop drinking. You will not have the willpower to fight temptation! In Matthew 16:24, Jesus having just taught on the mountain of Galilee, and thus arriving on the coast of Caesarea Philippi after performing many miracles, told His disciples, **"If any man will come after me, let him deny himself, and take up his cross and follow Me."** Beloved, we as Christians are Jesus' modern day disciples! That means that you have to put all your wants, desires, and needs aside, give up your life as you know it, and *accept* God's will for your life. In turn, God will perform miracles atop your spiritual mountain; helping you to become your highest and best self!

I would say sin at its root, derives from selfishness. The Bible says people are led away from God because of their own lusts (James 1:14). This verse is so powerful because if it were truly obeyed, how many would have forgone destroying their lives and families because of selfishness. Furthermore, if someone you dearly love, admire and respect–your muse–gives you a very expensive and precious gift and tells you to protect it and guard it with your life, would you not put said gift in a very safe place and cherish it dearly? Well beloved, that gift is your life! It was given to you by God! 1 Corinthians 6:19-20, says that your body is the temple of the Holy Spirit and you are not your own! I love how it eloquently goes on to state: **"For ye are bought with a price: therefore glorify God in your body, and in your spirit, which are God's."**

You are only a temporary occupant here on earth until your body returns to the dust, and your soul is claimed–either by God or by satan. But many are profaning, perverting, mutilating, prostituting, murdering and destroying God's property. Pro-Choice supporters are pushing the agenda that "a woman has a right to choose" to kill an unborn child in her womb, when her body is not even her own! Moreover, flip open many of today's magazines and you will find a host of articles targeting men, women and young girls with sexual oratory; highlighting such topics as "How to have hot sex," or "How to satisfy yourself" by learning to masturbate. What this is really teaching society is how to sin against one's own body and debase God's Holy Temple. Masturbation opens up the spirit to all types of perversion: fantasizing, fornication, pornography, adultery, rape, incest, bestiality. If Matthew 5:28, says to even look at a woman with a lustful intent is sin, surely masturbating is. In the Bible, the book of Song of Solomon, precariously tells the reader that love should not be stirred up or aroused until it pleases (*SOS 2:7, 8:4*). What it is saying is that sexual desire should not be acted upon until consummated with another (spouse). When a person masturbates there is some form of lustful desire or illicit thoughts (of a desired person or object) fueling the act which goes against the very word of God to be pure.

Additionally, when a man and woman consummate their relationship, the act of sexual intercourse is what creates their bond, or spiritual soul tie if you will (more on this topic in chapter 36*)*. God created sex for a purpose and function. It was not designed to be used selfishly or frivolously outside of a covenant relationship. Driving the point home, the Bible says that wasting semen displeases the Lord! Genesis 38:6-10, tells the story of a father named Judah who had two sons: Onan and Er. Judah tells his son Onan to sleep with his brother Er's widow to impregnate her to carry on Er's lineage. And you thought soap opera's were invented in the 20th Century. Ha! The Bible says that Onan was angst because the children would not belong to him, so when he had intercourse with Er's widow, he let his semen spill on the ground. Verse 38:10, says that this greatly displeased the Lord, so God killed him! God did not kill Onan because He favored his brother Er more; verse 38:7, says God killed him because he was wicked and disobedient! God created sex to be a covenant between husband and a wife in the context of marriage (Genesis 2:24). It is the very reason sex outside of this structure often contributes to unwanted pregnancy, broken homes, abortion, sexual diseases, and single-parent households.

Moreover, sex was designed for procreation. Onan spilling his seed was an act of disobedience and rebellion towards God. God favored many of the prophets by blessing their seed so that it would carry on His lineage from generation to generation to continue the work of the Gospel. The Bible tells us that Abraham was the father of many nations. God tells Abram (name before God changed it) in Genesis 17:7, **"I will establish my covenant between me and thee and thy seed after thee in their generations for an everlasting covenant, to be a God unto thee, and to thy seed after thee."** Abraham's seed produced Issac, whose seed then produced Jacob. More, God blessed Elizabeth to bear the great John the Baptist. God Blessed Hannah to bear the great prophet Samuel. God honored Jesse's (King David's father) seed as Heir to Jesus Christ himself! Moreover, "God blessed Noah and his sons, and said unto them, 'Be fruitful and multiply, and replenish the earth'" (Gen 9:1).

The people of that land deviated from God's original plan of procreation, and choose to live promiscuously, worship idols and fulfill their own lustful desires (Genesis 6:1-12). Just as God blessed nations and people, he also cursed immoral, idolatrous nations. It was the very reason God told Noah to build the Arc because He was very frustrated with the people had He created on earth because of their perversion and wickedness so He destroyed it. God also destroyed another wicked nation which was Babylon. Like Noah, God preserved Lot and his lineage by commanding Lot to flee with his family. But dismally, Lot's wife looked back, disobeying God's orders, and was turned into a pillar of salt. God destroyed this nation because of its evil, perversion and idolatry. But for one nation, there was hope! God commanded Jonah to go to Nineveh to announce His judgement against it because of its wickedness and evil. The Bible says that the people of Nineveh believed God, proclaimed a fast and put on sackcloth; from the greatest of them to the least of them (Jonah 3:5). When the king of Nineveh heard the warning that God was going to destroy the land in forty more days, he heeded God's word, took off his royal robes, commanded a fast, and "called urgently on God!" And God did not destroy that land! How about you? Will you heed God's voice before it's too late? Or will you gamble with your soul and take a chance by refusing to serve God? Beloved, when your soul leaves this earthly plane there will be no turning back, no more second chances. Is the sin you're indulged in worth going to hell for?

Trusting God

God says, "I will never leave you nor forsake you" (Deu 31:8). Let his verse comfort and reassure you. Your family may turn their backs on you, your mate may leave you, and your friends may walk out on you; but our Heavenly Father gives you His word that no matter what you go through, He will never leave you! You pray, and read your Bible, yet somehow you still allow satan to lead you to sin. You feel like you're living a lie: proclaiming the Gospel, but yet defeated in your life. Some of you may be asking if you are even a Christian! This verse reminds you that as a Christian you will make mistakes, but God won't give up on or walk out on you!

Romans 3:23, reminds us that we all have sinned and fallen short of the glory of God. You try to do your best, but to avoid a lot of needless guilt and self judgement, you must know that you are going to make mistakes, mess up, say the wrong things, and hurt people. It is all a part of growing. But, instead of indulging in self-pity, pick yourself up, ask God for forgiveness, and recite Deuteronomy 31:8: **"My God shall never leave nor forsake me!"** Recite it until it is ingrained in your psyche, until you believe it from the depths of you soul! Beloved, you have to believe it. If you find that you are going through some very painful situations right now and are hopeless, just keep repeating it until your faith catches up with your words!

What power do you have in knowing that you have a merciful God who loves you, and who bears with your sins as you grow in Christ! Amen! You have the power of the universe at your disposal! Other religions do not have that! All they have are dead idols, "positive thinking" mantras, affirmations, and chants. We have a *Person* who is alive and hears our prayers, heals our afflictions and contends with our enemies! That person is Christ, and yet most God-fearing people refuse to tap into that power! Just imagine your earthly father telling you that whatever you do, or whatever mistakes you make, he will always stand by your side and support you, no matter what situation you find yourself in. Wouldn't you feel infinitely loved, assured and secure? Beloved, that's how God operates in spirit! Most people give up on themselves too easily. To perfect anything there must be trial, error and failure; and with that comes learning from your mistakes, becoming better, and growing. It is no different being a Christian. But the beauty of it is, you have help from above! You do not have to go through life feeling alone. You have an all-knowing, all-powerful God available to you at all times! But herein lies the problem that limit many people from receiving this power: they don't believe that God is capable to do exceedingly above anything they can ask or think (Ephesians 3:20).

I was crippled by my unbelief for many years. I heard all the sermons, said all the Christian slogans, but still did not believe God would do it for *me*! I did not believe God would deliver me, heal me or bless me. Deep down inside I really did not believe God heard me. Half of the time I didn't bring requests to God in prayer because I did not have enough faith to believe He would answer them. Born into a very dysfunctional family, I just felt that my family was too cursed to be blessed, or that God forgot about me. I remember I used to always sing this Yolanda Adams song: *Even Me*. The gist of the song reiterated: Lord, while you are blessing, don't forget about me; "Even me, Lord." For a while that was my theme song. I often sang it with tears streaming down my face and my voice cracking, pleading with God out of desperation to change my situation. It *seemed* as if God was blessings other people just not me! Beloved, it's easy to look on the outside of people's lives and assume. The reality is, you really don't know what sacrifices people are making to God behind closed doors, which causes God's favor to overflow in their lives. I had to admit, I was not obedient and faithful to God as I should have been, but was wondering why God wasn't blessing me.

It is so simple, yet so hard to do: trust God! We are afraid to give that situation or problem to God thinking we know best how to handle it ourselves. If that were so, you wouldn't be in the situation you are in now. You may fear that if you let it go you are losing control, or you are going to be vulnerable. The Bible says, trust God with your whole heart and lean not on your own understanding (Proverbs 3:5). It's time for you to let go of whatever you are struggling with! You have been dealing with it long enough. Lift the burden off of yourself and hand it over to God–it's too heavy! Believe that He will heal your hurt. Fulfill your dream. Deliver your spouse. Bring back your prodigal child. Mend your heart. Heal your womb. Believe! And wait for your miracle!

Hebrews 11:1 says, **"Faith is the substance of things hoped for the evidence of things not seen."** I like how the writer of this verse states that faith is a substance, like it is tangible and can be grasped. Faith is something that you have to take hold of, it has to be concertedly grasped in your mind. There will be many storms in your life; better to make a concrete decision to trust God wholeheartedly no matter what situations you face. The sooner you acclimate yourself to this discipline of thinking, the easier it will be to get through the bad times. I didn't say it would be easy; no pain is easy, but if you can train your mind to know that whatever the outcome of the situation, ultimately God is in control and He has your greater good in mind. If I could have just learned that much earlier, it would have saved me a lot of grief and tears. Years ago as a spiritually immature Christian, people would tell me: "You gotta have faith," when I was going through something. I had received what they said, but I just did not know how to apply it; tap into it, turn it on. I began to think that it was just a cliché church folks said. All I had were problems, sickness, bills, stress, no money, heartache and pain...did I mention no money? My problems were like Goliath when he told the Israelites in 1 Samuel 17: 8, "Why don't you come out and line up for battle?" While I was like Celie from the movie, *The Color Purple* when her sister Nettie told her to fight her husband, Mister, back and she replied, "I don't know how to fight!" That was me, sobbing and crying just the same!

But, as I went through each tough situation, one-by-one I began to see how God gave me the strength to endure, or how He worked it out. Some of those situations were nothing short of a miracle! Having been delivered from trial after trial, I began to gain confidence like young David when he was a shepherd boy and God gave him strength to kill a lion and a bear, then ultimately the giant Goliath. With rocks of faith in my hand, I am now able to face my Goliath's. With each coming battle, I throw my stone of faith and proclaim as David did in 1 Samuel 17:37, **"The Lord, who delivered me from the paw of the lion and from the paw of the bear, He will deliver me from the hands of the Philistine."** And that beloved, is what I stand on this very day! No matter what battle rages against you, God will deliver you out of the hand of your enemy!

Truly Repent

Sadly, some people are their own worst enemies! A lot of times people blame God, or more so the devil for situations they very well have gotten themselves into. As I stated earlier, God gives us free will to make our own choices, however, He also gave us the Holy Spirit to convict us when we are doing things that are contrary to the word of God. To disobey this conviction is rebellion. If God tells you not to do a thing and you keep on doing it because you enjoy, or find pleasure in it, that is a choice *you* are making, so no one is to blame but yourself. God will honor your choice and allow all consequences of those sins. If you choose to disobey the heeding of the Lord, you will find yourself right in the midst of the devil's playground, uncovered spiritually in a dark and evil world.

The Bible asks in 2 Corinthians 6:14, what does righteousness and wickedness have in common? If you do not decide to walk away from people or activities that are not pleasing to God, you will bring destruction upon your own self. Yet woefully, a lot of Christians tread this tight rope! Many people love the sin that they are in and refuse to give it up! You have to make a choice; you have to decide if you love God, or the sin more. If you truly love

God more than your carnal desires, you have to separate yourself from people, things, places and situations that are keeping you in bondage. Yes, you will lose people whom you thought would always be there for you, you may have to leave a career that is dear to you, you will be lonely, and, you will cry–a lot.

Jeremiah 18:3 (ESV)

So I went down to the potter's house, and there he was working at his wheel. And the vessel he was making of clay was spoiled in the potter's hand, and he reworked it into another vessel, as it seemed good to the potter to do. Then the word of the Lord came to me: 'Oh house of Israel, can I not do with you as this potter has done? declares the Lord. Behold, like the clay in the potter's hand, so are you in my hand, O house of Israel.

In the above verses, God pleads through Jeremiah to the people of Jerusalem to turn from their evil ways. God is saying that although you are feeble, frail and imperfect like the spoiled clay, He is meticulously crafting your life in His hands! He knows the inner most wicked secrets of your heart and the fragmented parts of your personality. He is just asking you to live for Him, and He will use all of the broken pieces of your life and rebuild it into a beautiful vessel:

2 Timothy 2:21

If a man therefore purge himself from these, he shall be a vessel unto honor, sanctified, and meet for the master's use, and prepared unto every good work.

IT'S NOT TOO LATE!

Moreover, there are others who are not *willfully* sinning, but are struggling with a particular sin, or may have backslid into sin. Maybe you once had an intimate relationship with God, but now seem far away from Him, God still loves you despite of! Be honest and open with Him. Admit your trespasses, repent and ask God to renew your heart. Ask Him to help you with your sin, but most importantly, **wait on His deliverance!** That's the hard part, many break right before they're about to breakthrough. God is working it out according to His timetable, not ours. Sometimes God may prolong an area of weakness in your life to build a greater testimony in you! He's equipping you to help someone else who is going through what you went through or so He can get the glory!

While you are waiting on your deliverance, this is how you fight attacks: every time you are tempted by negative thoughts, depression, sadness or feel like giving up, research and write down helpful scriptures on a card. Carry it with you, and throughout the day recite the verses. Every time you are attacked emotionally, keep meditating on the verse until the bad thought and emotion that accompanies it leaves your mind. Most importantly, replace the bad thought/news with a good thought. You can't focus on negative and positive thoughts at the same time! Speak aloud a positive outcome that you would like to happen in your life; reversing the bad thought! That's called prophesying over your life. This is how you get deliverance! Practice doing this every time these types of situations occur, and slowly you will start to see that you are gaining power over these problem areas in your life. Your deliverance will not happen overnight, but you must be patient and not give up!

Be Still And Know That I Am God

I love the morning time! It's the time of day I'm most refreshed, productive and creative. For me, it's the time when I hear God's voice most clearly and feel His presence most profoundly. Sometimes as I start my day's journey, I'm in awe of the early morning dew, how it lovingly hugs the ground as a mother her child; the sweet melodies of birds as they hum along, each note tenderly caressing my ears; and the wind's breeze as it gently kisses my face. That's how God communicates with me! If you want to know if God is real, all you have to do is simply ask! In John 14:14, *God says,* **"If you ask anything in My name, I will do it!"** Amen!

Below are three profound stories of how I felt God's presence in my life:

God's Love

One morning, I was awakened out of sleep with a certain song in my spirit: *I am not forgotten*, which is one of my favorite Christian songs! Frankly, it's not just the song, but a particular version of the song that touches my heart. This version is sang by a child. I love it because as a child who experienced a very traumatic childhood, I would often pray and ask God if He had forgotten about me. The child's voice in the song brings back memories of the conversations I would have with God. More, it's ironic that years later God would use a child–similar to the age I was when I used to cry out to Him–to send an answer to my childhood prayer! This song has gotten me through some pretty rough times in my life! So, every time I hear it, it's a reminder that when I was a child, God really didn't forget me! He was there all along, and He had a plan for my life!

So before my foot hit the floor, I'm singing and humming along: *I am not forgotten*...as I'm getting ready for work. As part of my morning worship routine I listen to satellite radio. I started thinking as I continued to get dressed, really wondering why I had never heard *my version* playing on the radio before. I momentarily think about the song: how much it fills my heart with joy to hear, and how it makes me feel like God sits me on His lap, holds me in His arms, and tells me how much He loves me! *Oh well!* I shrug it off as not to spoil my joyous mood; still singing, I go to turn on the radio. To my surprise, what was playing? You guessed it–MY VERSION! Not only was it playing; it was playing in sync to the exact line in the song that I was singing! Amazing! I just could not believe it, so much so, I sat down on the bed and started crying! It was as if the Father woke me up that morning to specifically tell me that *I am not forgotten*, and to give me a hug from Heaven!

<u>God's Voice</u>

I've often heard stories about people whom profess to have had a human to supernatural encounter with God. I've heard some preachers preach about it, and lately there's been an influx of movies telling survivors' stories about their encounters with God. One day as I was reading a particular Christian book, I had gotten to the chapter where the protagonist in the story met God. Even though the book was fiction, it was poignantly written with such realness and detail; drawing the reader in as if they were right there going through the journey with the character. That day, I just couldn't stop thinking about this man's meeting with God. The husband and father had a horrible tragedy happen in His family, and was losing the little faith that he had in God. God loved the man so much that He came down from heaven and met with him to explain why he had to go through some of the horrible things that he went through.

I just kept rolling that part of the book over and over in my mind. That night, with a heavy heart, I prayed and asked God why He had not shown himself to me in a realistic way. About a week later, one morning as I began to pray, something was different. I felt the presence of the Holy Spirit in a different way than usual. I felt a comforting peace surrounding me. I began to weep as I prayed. The room seemed tranquil and warm as I kept praying. All of a sudden, I hear a voice in my spirit. A soft, subtle voice. I was frightened. Nonetheless, I kept praying. So before I went any further I asked if it was God, and was reassured! I sat there on that bed and prayed, asking intimated questions that I needed answers to. I asked God questions that had been on my heart throughout the years and He answered them in a most reassuring way! How did I know it was God? Because many of the things that He told me has since come to pass; this book being one of them! I was so scared I started shaking, but humbled that God loved me enough to answer my prayer and meet with me in a heartfelt way! Now I too can say that I had an encounter with the true and living God!

God's Presence

When my godfather, LT, who raised my sister and I died, I was devastated. I had moved to New York from New Orleans two years prior after graduating from college, and never could have imagined that when I left, that would have been the last time I would see him. Trying to establish myself in a new city–a very expensive city might I add–I simply could not afford to fly back home. When I left the nest, I remember him wishing me well on my new journey and in my new dwelling. He told me that he loved me, and gave me a warm hug goodbye. When I received the devastating news that he died, I was crushed. I went through a range of emotions: anger, guilt, frustration, sadness. I came down on myself really hard thinking that I should have made my way back home.

Moreover, I had not achieved my professional goals yet. I wanted LT, who I had come to know as my father, to be proud of me, but he would never live to see it.

Throughout the years, I would always think about the values he instilled in me and the things that he taught me about life and the world. Often, I would weep just thinking about how this man, who was not my biological father, worked so hard to put a roof over me and my sister's head (along with his own children), and made sure we had decent clothing, food to eat, and our basic needs met. He was a hard working man. So much so, I would later learn that he died while on the job. I learned so much from him, most importantly: a strong work ethic, being responsible, and being accountable. And politics!–boy did he love to talk about politics!

One particular day while walking down a New York City street, I started thinking about my dad. I started to get really emotional and melancholy. I started thinking about his rantings about life being unfair, high taxes, corporate America, the African-American experience in the U.S., and life in general. I remember him fussing about bills, escalating gas prices and the economy. But my most vivid memory of my dad that day was of him working hard year in and year out to make ends meet. As a child it really doesn't register when your parents fuss and complain about money, but when you become a bill-paying adult, you go through some of the same hardships your parents went through. Only then can you sympathize. Sadly, I watched over the years the spiritual demise of a kind-hearted, generous, gregarious man; to what had become a person who had given up on himself, lost his will to live, and died in bitterness and anger. A soul that had not made God the head of his life: he would speak frequently about killing himself to my godmother. He was not a practicing Christian, and therefore died in his sins. I really don't even know if he accepted Jesus Christ as his personal savior. I don't know if he was agnostic, but I do know he was not an atheist.

So as I continue solemnly walking down the street, head hung low, tears parading down my face; it seems as if the concrete path that I'm walking along–to no particular destination–is turning more and more green. Suddenly, one little white butterfly appears. It gets my attention when it starts encircling me. *Humm…that's weird,* I remember thinking to myself. As I'm slowly pacing along, a hedge of grass is protruding so far out onto the sidewalk it seems as if it brushes against my arm to get my attention! Then, a swarm of white butterflies swirl around me in sync as if they are performing a recital of Tchaikovsky's *Swan Lake*. As I stop to stare in admiration, I notice I am standing in the midst of a cul-de-sac, sprouted with tall, green trees and a rainbow of beautiful, colored flowers. I feel a warm ray on my face, only to look up and see a pristine blue sky, with a big bright sun beaming down on me! It's like God ushered me into His healing garden! As I inhaled the beauty of it all, I stood there weeping; no longer from sadness, but from God's comforting love! He loves us so much that He cares about our most personal concerns! In those moments when we are grieved with sadness, heart broken, and feel all alone, God reminds us:

The Lord your God is in your midst, a mighty one who will save; He will rejoice over you with gladness; He will quiet you by His love; He will exult over you with loud singing.

Zephaniah 3:17

Beloved, the Bible says that God is not a respecter of persons. God can speak to you and through you as does anyone else! Sadly, some people believe that God only speaks through pastors, priests or clergy. In the Bible, God handpicked certain prophets to speak for Him, and some could only speak to God through a prophet. In the New Testament, God spoke through His son, Jesus (John 14:10), but at Pentecost Jesus said the Father will send a comforter: The Holy Spirit.

"And I will pray the Father, and He shall give you another Comforter, that he may abide with you forever; Even the spirit of truth; whom the world cannot receive, because it seeth him not, neither knoweth him: but ye know him; for He dwelleth with you, and shall be in you. I will not leave you comfortless: I will come to you. Yet a little while, and the world seeth me no more; but ye see me: because I live, ye shall live also. At that day ye shall know that I am in my Father, and ye in me, and I in you. " John 14:16-20 (KJV).

Isn't it awesome that we are living in a time when we can talk to God directly, as opposed to having to speak to Him through an interpreter! God does speak Beloved! But in order to hear His voice we have to tune into His spirit! How do you do that? First, believe! Believe that you can hear from God and that He can speak to and through you! One of the worst mistakes young Christians make is not having enough faith to believe that they can hear from God! Second, prioritize your day to allow sufficient time to spend with God. He reciprocates to those who come to Him openly in prayer and reading His word. When you make it a daily habit to study God's word, you start to learn God's character and His heart. This is what will get you through life's storms: building yourself up on solid Biblical foundation. Third, after your prayer time, don't be in such a rush to get up and leave. Bask in His presence for a moment, see what comes into your mind, or presses upon your heart. Many times God has given me ideas, answers, information, told me how to handle difficult situations, or instructed me to call businesses or people that blessed me, just by sitting in His presence! Sometimes in prayer, God would put a person on my heart; many times I have picked up the phone to dial a friend or loved one and they were dialing me at the same time! Either they were going through something, or I was going through something and needed encouragement.

In closing, what I have found true is that God's voice is very subtle. Sometimes it may be a feeling that enamors you, an intuition, or a yearning in your spirit. I have had several occasions where God has used people to speak into my life. How did I know it was God? Because on each occasion the person reiterated to me what God had pressed upon my heart in the prayer closet. God speaks to people through visions, dreams, prophets, songs, the Bible, or any other method He deems necessary to relay a message or to get your attention. If God used a donkey to speak to Balaam in Numbers 22:28, surely He has many ways to communicate with His children. But, there is a Caveat Emptor: the Bible says in the last days there will be many false prophets. Loved one, if you don't spend time with God to hear His will for your life directly from Him, you may fall victim to a wrong spirit. When you pray, you will already know what God has told you, so if someone comes to you telling you, "God said", you will know the spirit of truth from a spirit of error! (1 John 4:1).

The Wedding

Welcome to *"The Wedding!"* Today's ceremony will be officiated in part by Pastor Paul from Tarshish.

PASTOR PAUL: Celebrate as I join *A Groom* and His beloved bride in Holy Matrimony!

CHORUS: We're going to chapel and we're gonna get m*a*a*ar*ried! We're going to the chapel of *His Love!*

WEDDING GUESTS: Let us be glad and rejoice and give Him glory, for the marriage of the Lamb has come, and His wife has made herself ready. Revelation 19:7.

PASTOR PAUL: For I'm jealous for you with godly jealousy. For I have betrothed you to one husband, that I may present you as a chaste virgin to Christ. 2 Corinthians 11:2.

BRIDE: My wedding dress is beautiful! "And to her it was granted to be arrayed in fine linen, clean and bright, for the fine linen is the righteous acts of the saints." Revelation 19:8.

BRIDE: A bride adorns herself with her jewels. Isaiah 61:10.

GROOM: For He has clothed me with the garments of salvation, He has covered me with the robe of righteousness. Isaiah 61:10.

GROOM: A bridegroom decks himself with ornaments. Isaiah 61:10.

GROOM'S SPEECH: You have ravished my heart, my sister, my spouse; You have ravished my heart with one look of your eyes, With one link of your necklace. Song of Solomon 4:9.

BRIDE'S SPEECH: As for me, I will see your face in righteousness; I shall be satisfied when I awake in your likeness. Psalm 17:15.

PASTOR PAUL: (Commencing ceremony) I now pronounce you man and wife! **"And you are Christ's, and Christ is God's."**
1 Corinthians 3:23.

Oh…and Phat Johnny...of course he got drunk and tried to ruin the wedding! Ephesians 5:18.

The Love Train

Welcome aboard the Love Train! We will be stopping at three life-changing destinations. So sit back, relax and enjoy the ride!

CONDUCTOR: Now arriving at our first stop: **FORGIVENESS**.

An arguing couple gets on, an estranged mom and her son gets on, and lastly, a rape survivor boards.

CONDUCTOR: It's a little stuffy inside passengers; open the windows of your heart! The second stop is a long ride: **LONGSUFFERING**.

CONDUCTOR: It's going to get a lil' tough but hold on!

A mom with an autistic child gets on, a cancer patient boards, followed by a drug addict.

CONDUCTOR: Ok passengers, last stop before we go express: **COMPASSION**.

Lucy and her little brother Phat Johnny get on the train bickering, a CEO pushes his way on while scowling at a homeless man begging for money. Lastly, a group of teens get on bullying a disabled peer.

CONDUCTOR: Thank you all for boarding the love train, where Jesus is the operator and heaven is the final destination!

What Is My Calling?

As Christians, we may sometimes feel like we aren't doing enough for the Kingdom of God, witnessing to enough souls, or handing out enough gospel tracts. This may leave you feeling seemingly out of place in the movement of God or oftentimes riddled with guilt. There may be an area in ministry that you are contemplating joining, but you have so much uncertainty: "What ministry should I join? Is it God's leading? What exactly is God's call on my life?" Guilt consumes you as you frustratingly try to figure it out. These are but a few of the questions I have asked myself over the years while walking with Christ. Many people are unsure of what role God would have them fulfill in the Kingdom of God. I ultimately felt that my calling was on the mission field because that's what I have always been drawn to. So I prayed, sought God, and waited—impatiently might I add—then God showed me that my calling is right where I am! In this season, my mission field is not all the way over on the other side of the world, but right here! My mission field is my relationships, the people I encounter on a daily basis, my community, and most importantly, my mission field is myself!

Beloved, when I started praying for what God would have me to do, my simplistic Christian life began to take a dramatic turn. God is not going to give you necessarily what you want, but what you need. A lot of Christians are praying, asking God to use them, but simply, some need deliverance from internal strongholds that may handicap their faith walk, or they have not been perfected in their gifts to be an effective witness for Christ. God has to allow you to go through training ground; spiritual warfare to be able to defeat the challenges that lie before you! In your naivety, you may think you are ready and prepared to do what's tugging at your heart. Credulously, when we pray we expect God to drop the answer down from heaven in a cute, neat little package: "Faith? You got it, now go walk in it! Patience? Granted! You can now suffer long, go and be at peace!" If it were that easy! Beloved, when you go to God with requests, God doesn't just instantly drop them down from heaven, you have to go through some hills and valleys before that prayer is answered.

I went through many trials and life-changing situations to prepare me for where I am today. There were things in my spirit that I didn't even know I needed to be delivered from, that God exposed to me! God allowed difficult times and times of testing to teach me and to build my character. And can I tell you beloved, many times my prayers for deliverance were answered, and my petitions granted without me even realizing it! The prayer that I prayed: *to be used by God*, did not show up the way that I thought it would, but nonetheless, God answered it in a way that glorified His name! This reminds me of the time in the book of Acts, when after three days Jesus descended from heaven and the Apostles asked Him about restoring Israel:

He said to them, "It is not for you to know times or seasons that the Father has fixed by his own authority. But you will receive power when the Holy Spirit has come upon you, and you will be my witnesses in Jerusalem and in all Judea and Samaria, and to the end of the earth" (Acts 1:7, 8). Beloved, God is saying we are not to question how or when He will use us, but we must remain open and willing to go and do His will when we are called. We will then be aided by the Holy Spirit to witness to those He puts in our path. **One who is faithful in a very little is also faithful in much, and one who is dishonest in a very little is also dishonest in much (Luke 16:10).**

I was so ready to go serve on a mission field so far away, but God showed me that there are souls dying here, right next to me on the fields of sin. During a long season, I found myself witnessing to an influx of broken hearted, lost people; those desiring to know God, as well as those rejecting God! And let me just tell you most of those situations showed up as problems, cantankerous people, stress, and contention. Naturally, when you meet any kind of resistance you want to run in the other direction. But saints if you avoid all people who exhibit obstinate traits, you run the risk of a missed opportunity to introduce Christ. Instead of running away from difficult situations or people, pray and ask God to give you provision regarding the situation and ask for a greater measure of patience.

Many people often forfeit growing spiritually, building character, or allowing God to use them by running away from their problems. If you are ever going to serve in a larger capacity in ministry, or in life for that matter, the difficult people around you now are your training ground. Don't run away from them! Pray and trust God to work out His salvation in their lives and yours too. Ask God to perfect your love language and teach you how to effectively relate to people. Don't be moved! Pray for His will to be done in the lives of people that are in your inner circle. You are there at that company, in that family, in that situation for an appointed reason! God has you there for a purpose: His divine plan! God is preparing you for a ministry, don't stunt your growth!

If you feel you haven't yet found your calling, maybe God has to see if He can use you right where you are first, before he can graduate you! He needs to see if you are going to be faithful to the few around you, before He can give birth to your God ordained calling!

A Soliloquy Of Love's Consuming Fire

A Soliloquy of Love's Consuming Fire.
In 4 acts:

Seven times hotter was the order for Shadrach, Meshach & Abednego. The fire didn't touch them, but it was burning inside their soul!

Then Nebuchandnezzar was full of fury, and the expression on his face changed toward Shadrach, Meshach, and Abed-Nego. He spoke a command that they heat the furnace seven times more than it was usually heated. Daniel 3:19

Christ is *not* just Christmas, with its festivities, decorated lights, or even a shining star atop a tree. His fire is alive everyday and His light burns inside of you and me!

For our God is a consuming fire. Hebrews 12:29

When the waters rise, I'll ride on its tides. When I walk through the flames not even one hair on my head will be maimed!

When you pass through the waters, I will be with you; and through the rivers, they shall not overwhelm you; when you walk through fire you shall not be burned, and the flame shall not consume you. Isaiah 43:2

But His word was in my heart like a burning fire shut up in my bones; I was weary of holding it back, and I could not. Jeremiah 20:9

Christian Seasons

Just as weather seasons, as a Christian, you too will go through various changes throughout your life; some good, and some bad. I went through a season in my Christian walk when I had slipped back into some of the behaviors God had delivered me from, and did not feel the joy and excitement I once felt when I first got saved. In astonishment and great disappointment, I became very down on myself wondering how did I get to this point. When you first become born again, you have been delivered and set free from satan's hold over you. An overwhelming feeling of joy, peace and the Father's love floods your hearts. It is a spiritual high! Some foolishly think that they have won the battle and there is no more fighting left to do! So off they go living life trying to sustain on this one-time feeling of euphoria! Just like a drug addict when a high wears off, and the harsh realities of life abound, they go looking again for that "first fix." Some Christians seek out every prayer group, Christian conference, and/or self-help book they can find, while asking everyone they know to pray for them in search of this nostalgia! Others may have given their lives to God out of desperation expecting a quick fix, but when their problems weren't solved immediately, they undoubtably walked away from God and declared that this Christianity stuff does not work!

But the one who endures to the end will be saved.

Matthew 24:13 (ESV)

Those who have lost the joy that they experienced when they first became saved and are trying to find it again, are on the right path! They may not know to what extent just yet. Some people think that after becoming born again, the

Christian walk is more about religion or legalism. But in actuality, that peek into heaven they experienced; that overflowing joy they are seeking, is a personal relationship with Jesus! I'm not just talking about knowing who Christ is, but having a type of relationship with Him where you feel like He is a mother, a father, a caregiver, or a best friend; having a personal, intimate relationship with Him where you can talk freely and openly to Him and are assured that He hears you! Hallelujah! *He is* the Everlasting High! And those that seek Him will find him!

When you become born again, some strongholds will immediately be broken off your life, others will take months, perhaps even years, with God's grace. But what about when you have been saved for some time, have a personal relationship with Jesus, yet still fall back into sins you have already been delivered from? Maybe as you are reading this right now you are intensely struggling in your spiritual walk and your worship seems lackluster. Or, perhaps you are suffering intense persecution from the devil and you feel no joy at all! Why does God allow this to happen even though you may be seeking His face, praying and reading your Bible? Let's look at some possibilities:

GROWTH

1. God is growing you spiritually. After you have accepted Jesus Christ as your personal savior, you are termed "born again," meaning you have experienced a "spiritual" rebirthing. You are as a new born baby entering into a new, unfamiliar spiritual world! As a babe in Christ, God will gently nudge you along. Over

time, while you are still learning how to walk spiritually, you will stumble and oftentimes fall. When you watch a toddler exploring its new surroundings, you will eventually see the child bumping into things, tripping, and curiously wandering into dangerous zones; oftentimes getting hurt or bruised–that's new Christians! And, just as an earthly father, God picks you up, dusts you off, and encourages you to keep on going! Eventually you will be strong enough to take steps on our own. With spiritual nourishment (learning the Bible), you will thus continue to grow to higher levels in Christianity. To become a powerful Christian, you must make a concerted commitment to keep learning and growing in Christ! If we define growth, it states: To increase by natural development, as any living organism or part by assimilation of nutriment; **increase in size or substance.** If you stick with it, and don't throw in the towel no matter what it may look like in the physical realm, you will naturally progress! You have to hold on to the promises of God, not judge what you see with your natural eyes or succumb to your fickle feelings. You grow as a Christian, not only by studying God's word, but by *applying* it to your life. There is also a supernatural aspect to your growth as a Christian. What may appear to be denials, closed doors, and disapprovals, will happen no matter how much you pray or fast. Rest assured, trying times will come, and God may even *seem* silent. He will test your faith with patience. Though many of the circumstances you go through are not understandable to you, God is meticulously crafting an original assignment that only *you* are equipped to complete! And, to gain the experience needed, there are several avenues you must take to gain the necessary life experiences needed to be proficient in this calling. Though these things will be hard to endure, it is the only way you will learn certain lessons. I cannot tell you how many times I've read my Bible, and did not fully comprehend a thing until I went through it! Supernatural growth increases your spiritual substance, and expands your spiritual learning far beyond what your mind can comprehend.

COMPLACENCY

2. Sometimes God blesses people and they become lazy or complacent. Christianity involves constant change, growth, stretching and learning. When you stop moving, you become spiritually stagnant. When you are not praying, fasting, and studying like you used to, your spirit is becoming more and more polluted with the world. God allows persecution and trials to cause you to fervently pray for a situation, or to pray for a person who is treating you badly because they may not have anyone else praying for them. Also God may allow persecution to get your attention! When you become complacent you are slowly giving ground back to the enemy! Sadly, once saved, some expect God to do all of the work for them! The Bible says faith without works is dead (James 2:20). More so, in the event of a tragedy, some people become very angry with God, and question His love. Some may have lost

a loved one and ask: "God, where were You when my son died?" But God is at the very same place He was when His own son–Jesus–died! Right there in your heart! He loved you so much that He allowed *His* only begotten Son to die so that you could live! Beloved, if you neglect to pray, talk to, and press in to know God for yourself, you will never deeply experience this love He has for you!

UNREPENTANT SIN

3. Is there a pleasurable sin in your life and you refuse to let go of it? Sin hinders answered prayers. I'm not speaking about sin you're genuinely struggling with, but sin that you have made excuses for and refuse to turn over to God. What I find today is that, many use God's grace as an excuse to sin. Because God is such a merciful God, some are refusing to turn away from behavior that God has specifically warned will bring destruction upon oneself. In today's generation, there is hardly a reverence or fear of God. People believe that "God understands" their sin and there will be no repercussions for their behavior. People are having sex outside of wedlock, involved in wrong relationships and are co-habituating before marriage (many are Christians). But the ones who remain faithful till marriage are deemed strange! Beloved, God is a merciful God, but He will only give you so long to repent and turn from sin. Egotistically, humans think they're going to live forever, but some end up dying in their sin! Don't let that be you! Repent and turn away

from things that are not pleasing to God, lest you become consumed in your transgressions. Many people go to great lengths to insure their property and valuables, but neglect to insure their most valuable property: their soul.

<u>A LOVELESS WALK</u>

4. A loveless walk is a person who is walking with (serving) God, yet does not love people the way God commands; refusing to exercise the fruits of the spirit: love, joy, peace, patience, kindness, goodness, faithfulness (Galatians 5:22). Persons who refuse to embrace a spirit of love towards the people they come into contact with on a daily basis; refusing to be kind and tolerant towards people in their life. A loving walk means being loving, kind, generous, patient and forgiving those who have hurt, rejected, or mistreated you. You cannot in your own strength do this. It will take a lot of prayer and study in the area of forgiveness, but most importantly, it will take God's grace! It may take many years before you are free; before you can forgive someone else, but you must be patient with yourself. Instead of praying vengeance upon a person, your thinking must switch over to praying for the person's soul (Matthew 5:44). The pain that they have caused you hurts terribly, therefore, you must begin to pray for your heart (Psalm 51:10), and their salvation. If you want to have a life of spiritual freedom and joy in Christ, this is the key that unlocks the door to your heart to be able to love people with

God's love!

EASILY OFFENDED

5. This is an area so hidden in the heart of many Christians that they are not even aware that it is a major hinderance to answered prayer. Offense is defined as: **A cause of transgression or wrong.** Therefore, offense can be further explained as when a person offends, hurts, mistreats or wrongs someone and the receiver holds a grudge or grievance against the perpetrator. Being easily offended is furthermore best described as persons who are so fragile, or insecure that constructive criticism, comments, critique, or behavior by others are *perceived* as a threat or an offense. Sometimes the offender's behavior may be valid. Nonetheless, holding a grudge because of an offense caused by another is so detrimental to the church body that it causes anger, hatred, strife and division amongst members. Furthermore, offense utterly destroys homes, families, friendships, and relationships. When you harbor grievances against people, you put up a spiritual wall. Slowly, you build a barrier of protection–hurt by hurt–around yourself, refusing to release love in fear of being hurt again. Most importantly, what many people do not realize is, the wall that they have built to block people out is also the same wall that is preventing God's love from entering in. Consequently, bitterness, anger, and hatred, which has no other place to go, manifests inside the body as sickness and disease.

SPIRITUAL MATURITY

6. Christianity is nothing more than a continuous spiritual classroom. God wants to graduate you to the next level in Him. Beloved, in order for anything you do to grow, you must grow! Whether it be a business, finances, relationships, or your very Christian walk! A word, deliverance, anointing, or breakthrough God has given you yesterday, you cannot live on today! You should be constantly learning and growing. When you have defeated satan in a certain area of your life, don't let your guards down! Can I tell you that the devil is working overtime trying to get you back into that bondage! He will send situations and people into your life to pervert the very word of God, attack the anointing on your life, outsmart, and relentlessly harass you! He fights a fierce battle trying to make you give up, give in and throw in the towel. So many of our saints have fallen by the waste side because they simply were not growing spiritually, therefore they were improperly suited for battle! The higher we go in God, the more we must learn in order to be one step ahead of our enemies. Ephesians 6:13, tells us to put on the whole armor of God!

Healing Balm Cafe's
Ten Commandments

1. **Thou shall pursue your calling**
Don't be afraid to take risks. If God has a specific calling on your life, have faith that He is going to manifest it and bless your dream.

2. **Thou shall not be afraid to fail**
You have to fail a few times before you can learn how to succeed in life. Don't believe the negative voices that tell you that you will never make it! Never give up on yourself and keep holding God's hand each step of the way until you reach your goals!

3. **Thou shall believe in yourself**
You must continue to climb life's mountain even when there seems to be no end in sight. There's going to be some rough and slippery terrain, but if you don't keep climbing, you will never know if you can make it all the way to the top!

4. **Thou shall not make others executors of your happiness**
Meditate on God; your joy comes from the Lord. People will disappoint, hurt, cheat and walk out on you, but how you *choose* to react makes all the difference. Choose to respond positively even though people may hurt you! Spend time with God, get to know Him intimately. Fall in love with Him so

you will be full of love already when you enter into relationships.

5. Thou shall seek peace in relationships
Be open to other people's ideas and meet them in the middle of the road. Accept constructive criticism without taking offense. Be quick to resolve a dispute...and always forgive!

6. Thou shall not worry about your life
Try not to worry about problems that arise. Put your trust in God! You'll have to *Go through* dark times, but God's light will always lead you out!

7. Thou shall be open to growing
Trials present opportunities to learn your behavior patterns and make necessary corrections, it also challenges you to be open to change. When you go through a difficult time try to find the lesson in it and learn from it!

8. Thou should not judge and/or be critical of others.
Try to see people through God's eyes. If someone is different than you that does not mean that they are better or inferior to you. God made us all different and unique, but we were all created in His image.

9. Thou shall not believe other people's opinions about you

Some people will not like you. Some will talk badly about and criticize you. Do not give people permission to validate who you are! God's opinion is the only approval you need.

10. Thou shall NEVER give up

Life can be challenging is an euphemism! Don't allow life's problem's to rob you of your joy! Every struggle in your life only makes you stronger to defeat the next one you will face! Every bad thing that has ever happened to you made you the beautiful person that you are today! Problems help you to stay close to God! Life is a gift; cherish it, nurture it, and it will bless you in return!

A mother's love

A Mother is sitting at the kitchen table reading the newspaper and enjoying her morning cup of coffee as her son plays outside near the garden, in which she told him not to touch. As she gets up to refresh her cup, little Johnny comes running into the kitchen. Looking up at her with his big brown eyes, he hugs her by the waist and says: "Mommy, I love you so much, do you love me?" Replies the mother, "Of course I love you son!" The mother is stunned and elated by her son's sudden dose of affection.

Smiling as she bends down to hug him; out of the window–to her dismay–she sees trampled roses strewn all across the yard, Johnny's muddy boot trail stamped across her kitchen floor, as decapitated tulips lay unearthed and lifeless in hindsight. More, the family's dog, spot, is buried helplessly in dirt.

The mother screams in horror, then scolds her son about the mayhem. "Where's the love mommy?" replies little Johnny, with a sad puppy dog face and crocodile tears struggling to fall. "Oh…poor baby," the mother says sarcastically, "It's in the corner waiting for you!"

Furthermore, we have had human fathers who corrected us, and we paid them respect. Shall we not much more readily be in subjection to the Father of spirits and live? For they indeed for a few days chastened us as seemed best to them, but He for our profit, that we may be partakers of His holiness. Hebrews 12:9, 10.

The Funeral

I was dead in Christ. I had to go to my own funeral. Oh, but when Jesus touched me it was a Holy Ghost Revival! Acts 1:8.

As a babe in Christ, I had given my life to God, but my mind was still in the world. But He touched me and that *old man* died, and my soul came alive! I was transformed, and He renewed my mind! Romans 12:2.

I was a *dead man walking* in the Lord for a long time, oh but then I met Jesus personally; I was resurrected from the grave of sin! Hallelujah! Ephesians 2:1-10.

I died once...but I was born twice! Romans 6:4.

When I was in the world the days were too long and too dark–and I wanted to die. Now that I'm in Christ the *Son* meets me every morning and gives me new life! Hosea 14:7.

Therefore if anyone is in Christ, he is a new creation. The old has passed away. Behold, the new has come! 2 Corinthians 5:17.

Gospel*mercial*

Announcer: We are sorry to interrupt your regularly scheduled reading time, but we are excited to inform you of an exciting new breakthrough!

Are you at a standstill in your prayer life? Do you feel like your prayers are hitting a blank wall? Are you spending valuable time in prayer but not seeing any results? **WELL HAVE WE GOT A SOLUTION FOR YOU...FASTING!!!** Fasting is easy and convenient, can be done at anytime of the day or night, and you can fast for as long or as short of a time as you want!

LET FASTING HELP YOU REACH YOUR PRAYER GOALS!!! FASTING IS PRAYER ON HIGH OCTANE! Get your blessings while they last!

If The Bible Is A Sword
...Fasting Is A Battle Ax!

Jesus was led up by the Spirit into the wilderness to be tempted by the devil. And after fasting forty days and forty nights, he was hungry. And the tempter came and said to him, "If you are the Son of God, command these stones to become loaves of bread." But he answered, "It is written, Man shall not live by bread alone, but by every word that comes from the mouth of God" (Matthew 4:1-4 ESV).

Every approaching year as you ponder your life, in retrospect, you compile a list; whether a mental or a physical list of things you failed at, things you would like to do better, or perhaps accomplishments you would like to achieve. Off you go–full steam ahead–making plans, buying "self-help" books, joining gyms, taking classes and the like. The new year always brings anticipation and encouragement! It gets the ball rolling under your feet and gives you a compass to plot your course. Looking back over your shoulder, you may find yourself not having accomplished nearly all that you had set out to. I have found myself at this place many a times. The problem is, we set out to tackle goals in your own strength. The Bible talks a great deal about the flesh. It emphasizes that the flesh is weak and unpredictable.

For I know that nothing good dwells in me, that is, in my flesh. For I have the desire to do what is right, but not the ability to carry it out (Romans 7:18 ESV).

I used to think, no wonder we can't get anything done! That is until I learned how to master a valuable spiritual tool: fasting! One day while at a drug store–while miserably on a fast might I add–I ran across a book simply titled: *Fasting,* by Jentezen

Franklin. God really does have perfect timing, and a sense of humor! In the book, Franklin talks about how his church goes on a 21-day Daniel Fast at the beginning of each year. For those of you who may not be familiar with what a Daniel Fast is, it is taken from the book of Daniel in the Bible. The prophet Daniel was exiled from Judah by order of Babylonian King Nebuchadnezzar, to reside in the king's palace. The king ordered what food was to be eaten by the exiles, but Daniel refused to defile himself by eating the King's royal food, instead petitioning the steward in charge of him, that he and three fellow servants would be as strong as the other youths eating only vegetables (Daniel 1:1-16, 10:2,3).

The principle of the Daniel Fast of course is to eat mostly vegetables, however different churches have different variations of the fast. For those of you that may be wondering what you can and cannot eat on the Daniel Fast, a quick Google search or a trip to the library should give you tons of information. Moreover, as I read along in the book, I began to get more and more encouraged reading the testimonies of the pastor's congregation and anecdotes of other christians who received miracles after having completed the fast. The tome inspired me to start incorporating the yearly Daniel Fast into my life! Beloved, it is one of the hardest, but most spiritually rewarding things I have ever done! Through fasting I have broken several strong holds and generational curses off my life, have abundant peace, and have a closer, more intimate relationship with God. I have outlined some areas that you may be struggling with that fasting is proven to help:

1. Spiritual attacks

If you feel you are under a heavy burden, have nightmares, or experiencing high levels of stress in your life, consider a fast! Sometimes our spirit can feel so heavy and our mind greatly perplexed, that we can't even pray! Fasting helps quiet the soul and allows you to hear God's voice more clearly. While on a fast, you will know when you get a breakthrough because you will experience an overwhelming sense of peace and contentment. Most times it happens during a fast, but there have been times when I did not feel that peace until after the fast was over. Your problem and worry will just fall off! The thing that bothered you will no longer have such a great impact! You will gain the strength you need to deal with problems you are facing and you will have more patience waiting on God.

Is not this the fast that I choose: to loose the bonds of wickedness, to undo the straps of the yoke, to let the oppressed go free, and to break every yoke? (Isaiah 58:6 ESV).

2. Temptation

If you are greatly tempted in an area of your life, consider fasting. You will not only be feeding your spiritual body, but starving your physical body of its cravings, habits, and desires. Many people who attempt to challenge temptation on their own effort fail miserably. Obliviously, they think it is willpower. "You can do anything you put your mind to," is the catchphrase of today's society. Yet, dreadfully many men and women are falling victim to debilitating addictions. Beloved, can I tell you it's a battle of the spirit and not of the flesh! Unless you began to attack the addiction from a spiritual standpoint, you will never win! **And those who belong to Christ Jesus have crucified the flesh with its passions and desires. If we live by the Spirit, let us also walk by the Spirit (Galatians 5:24, 25 ESV).** We crucify the flesh with fasting! When we choose to walk by the spirit, it helps us not to give in to the mind, habits, cravings, and desires. We in turn, are allowing the Holy Spirit to fight the battle of temptation on our behalf!

3. Decision making

Whenever you have a big decision to make, i.e. buying a house, car, or contemplating a business venture, considering marriage, moving, a new job, or whatever may be of importance to you, it is imperative that you fast before a commitment is made! How many times have you felt certain about a decision and then the next day changed your mind? You then go back and forth in your thoughts until you have worked up a headache! There are three voices speaking to us at any given time: ours, satan's, and God's. Fasting is the eliminator! It allows you to hear God's voice more clearly or better heed His will and direction for your life, and prevent you from making disastrous mistakes. Many times through fasting, God has told me not to go or move in a certain direction that I thought I wanted to move in, and later allowed me to see the traps that were set before me, or the grave mistakes I would have made.

4. Weight loss issues

Albeit, spiritual fasting is not for weight loss, but as servants of Christ, we must address issues of the body of Christ. Many women and men struggle to lose weight. Some have become greatly despondent and depressed because of years of yo-yo dieting, counting calories, following medical advice and still not being able to lose the weight. A lot of women who have had children complain that they cannot lose their baby fat. Additionally, some have been overweight since childhood, some have eating or emotional disorders, many have full-time jobs, and some have illnesses which causes weight gain. Whatever the situation, weight issues are subjective to each person, and it causes deep pain and sorrow to the ones affected by it. Countless people fail at their weight loss goals because in the long-term, they just can't seem to stick with it. Year after year, many join gyms, try fad diets, and put their hope and faith in a fat burner pill, only to find the few pounds that they have lost is regained, and then some!

Beloved, how about giving this problem to God? What have you got to lose but the weight? First, pray and ask God to help you with your weight loss goals. Then try diligently to incorporate fasting into your lifestyle. When you first start fasting, it will begin to train the body to eat less. If you can start disciplining the body to fast on a regular basis, you will find that it becomes easier as time goes by. The more you fast, the more pounds you will shed. Fasting is the quickest, healthiest form of weight loss if done properly. Moreover, fasting shrinks the stomach! Overtime, you will find that you are not able to eat as much food as you used to after a fast, which can greatly enhance your weight-loss efforts. Before you resolve to lose weight on yet another weight loss plan, how about considering a fast and asking God for His help and guidance? You'll not only tone up your physical body, but also your spiritual body as well!

5. Hearing God's voice more profoundly

I have noticed that when I fast, I can discern God's voice more clearly. All the mind's chatter, mental confusion, and mental clutter is quieted. Moreover, I have noticed it is a time when I have deeper intimacy and fellowship with God! When we nullify the process of eating, it allows the body to rest from the work and toil of processing food, therefore allowing the mind to receive information more clearly. Also, when fasting, one must be cautious of busyness. Ensure yourself accurate time to rest because initially your body will work overtime ridding itself of toxins, therefore, your strength may be depleted until your body removes waste and adjusts to the fast. Cut down on all extra-curricular activities and social outings as much as possible, and try to spend the time you are fasting in God's presence. Again, the goal of fasting is to isolate yourself from the the noise of world in order to hear from God in your spirit. In the beginning of my Christian life, there were things that I had prayed for that God did not answer right away, or things I was impatiently or begrudgingly waiting on that did not manifest until I learned how to humble myself before The Lord.

Example: There was one time I was living in a place where I had to move. Had to move! I prayed and prayed, months and months went by. I was at a point of desperation! At first, it didn't start as a fast, but worry! I was so worried about the situation that I couldn't eat. So, since I didn't have an appetite anyway, a thought came to me: *Why don't you just fast?* So I fasted for a period of time. At the end of the fast, I had a dream that I was standing in a two-bedroom apartment with white walls! I awoke thinking it was odd because I didn't have a family, so why would I be dreaming about a two-bedroom apartment? So I really didn't think much of the dream, and shrugged it off. It would be approximately 1 year later that I moved into a lovely apartment! There I was standing in the hallway with a direct view of two-bedrooms with white walls, when God reminded me of the dream! It was the exact vision He had showed me! And get this: I was praying for a one-bedroom apartment, and God blessed me with a two-bedroom apartment at the market value of the former! Hallelujah! Saints sometimes we just have to press into God–through fasting–and wait on His timing!

Ezra 8:23

So we fasted and earnestly prayed that our God would take care of us, and he heard our prayer.

This book of the law shall not depart from your mouth, but you shall meditate on it day and night, that you may observe to do according to all that is written in it. For then you will make your way prosperous, and then you will have good success.

~Joshua 1:8

Meditate On The Word

The devil had me in the death of its jaws with an iron-clad grip and would not let go! It seemed as if heaven were shut up! I could not understand it. Though I usually fasted, prayed and read the Bible, the warfare was not letting up! Does this scenario sound familiar to you? I am talking about a time in your Christian walk when you are going through a period of trials and persecution and have done all that you know how to do, yet still feel defeated. Up until this point I thought I had all my bases covered, but it wasn't until I was listening to a sermon one day about meditating on the word, that I got a breakthrough! I heard it said many times before, but this time it *stuck* in my spirit. *I read my Bible,* I thought to myself, *but what exactly is meditating on the word?* As I continued to listen, I realized I was not diligently *utilizing* the word of God. The more I thought about it, I could very well say that I read the Bible sporadically, and had only memorized a few ubiquitous verses: The Lord's prayer (Matthew 6:9-13), Psalm 23, and the Ten Commandments–to mention a few. After listening further, it finally sank in to *meditate* on the word! How do you do that and what does that exactly mean? I didn't know, but had a dogged determination to find out.

The Greek word for the verb *meditate* is hagah (pronounced 'daw-gaw'). It is an action word meaning to ruminate, roll over in the mind, analyze, study, imagine, muse, mutter and groan.

I was reminded of the book of James, verses 1:23-24, when it tells the parable of a man looking in a mirror at himself, then after going away, immediately forgets what he looks like. I admit, I would only read the Bible when I was stressed out, going through a tough situation, or when at church. I didn't even take notes on the sermon, or write down scriptures for that matter; the word went in one ear and out the other! When everything was going good in my life, I hardly ever picked up a Bible. I was indeed as James says in verse 1:22: a hearer of the word only, and not a doer of it! I did not put the word into practice. I would hear it, then go back to living life as usual. So what I gathered was that I needed to really spend time with the Bible and *study* it.

My first action of recourse was asking the Holy Spirit for guidance and wisdom before I began my study time. I then wrote down scriptures dealing with areas that I was struggling with in my life. Next, I bought different translations of the Bible and referenced scriptures between the different texts. This gave me a better understanding of the different expressions of the subtext. I also got a dictionary to look up words I didn't understand. This greatly enhanced my study time and ability to accurately assimilate the word of God.

For the Lord disciplines the one he loves, and chastises every son whom he receives (Hebrews 12:6 ESV).

I started to really study the Bible, but I wasn't very consistent. Most working class adults find it hard to incorporate study time when they have a full schedule, but the enemy will be sure to remind you when you fall off! His attacks are so calculating and cunning, and it comes so sudden, it knocks you off course! Instead of first putting on the armor Galatians 6:11-18 speaks about, you put on panic and fear, then go running to God with your tail between your legs like a wounded puppy, when God has already given you the tools needed to fight! I went through this cycle for years, no wonder I was always defeated! The tools won't work if you don't use them!

For though by this time you ought to be teachers, you need someone to teach you again the basic principles of the oracles of God. You need milk, not solid food (Hebrews 5:12 ESV).

I felt as if God were telling me, "Enough! How many times are you going to go through this stumbling block in your Christian walk before you learn?" What was it going to take for me to chomp down and bite into the "meat" of the word for my sustenance instead of still relying on the milk of the young, unlearned Christian? As God's people, when faced with trials you should not allow your first line of defense to be a defeated mentality and worry; but **faith**, **courage** and **fight!** You must use faith as your shield, courage as your strength, and God's promises as your artillery to fight back! Fight back by being prepared with scripture. Fight back by verbally canceling any attacks against you in the *Name of Jesus!* Fight back by not feeling sorry for yourself, but attacking your enemies with thus says the Lord! Fight back by claiming your blessings! Fight back by *meditating* on the word!

If you have a calling on your life; meaning God has specifically told you that you are to work in some capacity for Him, you must live a disciplined life! There is absolutely no way around it! The devil will attack you more fiercely because he wants to shut the mouth of God! In the battles of my darkness, this is the ammunition God was trying to equip me with! You may think the battle is over because you won a few skirmishes, but with each victory won, the enemy is plotting new territory! If you heed the Holy Spirit's prompting, there may be areas God is calling you to be more diligent in, in preparation for the work He will have you to do. And that diligence will require **fighting for your freedom!** If you are called in Christ, you will receive a great amount of persecution! If you do not study to show yourself approved, you will be defeated every time! It is a call to rise up to a higher level of discipline and unshakeable faith! God requires your time! Time that must be devoted to study instead of what the flesh wants to do, and to the yielding of the Holy Spirit to be led by Him!

How to meditate on the word:

1. **Ask The Holy Spirit for wisdom and understanding**

2. **Set aside daily prayer/study time**

3. **Practice quieting your spirit in order to learn how to hear God's voice**

4. **Bible study tools:**

    Bible

    Concordance Bible

    Dictionary

    Pen/ Paper

    Notebook/flash cards

Healing Balm Cafe: The Eulogy

Scene:

Everyone is gathered together at a funeral service.

AGAPE LOVE: Congregants, as we come together in unity this *new* day, let us all say good bye to someone we once loved dearly. As saints of God, He often calls us to let go of what was, and look ahead toward The Great Call that lies before us. I encourage you not to look at it as a loss, but a new beginning.

AGAPE LOVE: Tonight's program will be officiated by none other than Grandma Gospel, JC Reppa, and Fat Johnny.

GRANDMA GOSPEL: (Goes up to the podium...taps mic) Hello... (Pounds mic) Hel-LO!... (Screams into mic) HELLO!!!

JC REPPA: We can hear you!

---

*The dialect of these characters are written phonetically to capture the true essence of Southern dialect and urban street slang.

GRANDMA GOSPEL: Oh...oh...Dearly Beloveds, we are gathered here today for this thing called deathhh...

PHAT JOHNNY: (Interrupts) Granny Gums, what you preachin', a *Purple Rain* eulogy?

GRANDMA GOSPEL: Oh sorry son, had a flash back (reminiscing)...boy I tell ya, Prince was *"It"* back in the day! I tell ya we used to...boy...(starts singing and dancing): *"I would die for you...darlin' if ya want me to..."*

JC REPPA: (Screams) GRANNY! Get on with the funeral!!!

GRANDMA GOSPEL: Oh yea...oh yea...(clears throat). I would like to wish **SIN** a peaceful farewell! **CUSSIN'**, you had to go! **LYIN'**, now you know God had to kill your tongue! **CIGARETTES**...(screaming) I BIND YOU IN THE NAME OF JESUS! **WINE!**...oh wine...(starts weeping), I 'member those lonely nights we had...jus' me and you (nostalgic). I 'member the way you used to make me feel...boy...Granny used to get drunk as a skunk!!! Stanky drunk! Sloppy drunk! Funky drunk! (Sobs...) I 'member when no one was there for me but you!

(Screams) WINEEEE!...I LUVS YOU! (Dramatic) Ooh...wine, I hate to see you go! (Crying uncontrollably) Oh Laawd...my wine...(falls out onto a chair). My sweet, sweet wineeee! (Sobbing as ushers go up on stage and fans her).

JC REPPA: (Shouts) GRANNY! (Goes up on podium and grabs the mic). Excuse Granny, ya'll know she gets a lil' emotional. Moving right along...let us not forget why we are gathered here today.

PHAT JOHNNY: Preach Martin Luther! Preach! From the mountain top...(sings) to the v-a-l-l-e-y low (baritone voice).

JC REPPA: (Gives Phat Johnny a piercing look).

PHAT JOHNNY: Oh, I'm sorry bruh! My bad...my bad!

JC REPPA: Like I was sayin'...first I want to thank my Lord and Savior Jesus Christ. If it had not been for Him, I wouldn't be here today!

PHAT JOHNNY: Man, this ain't no BET awards show!

GRANDMA GOSPEL: (Falling out of her pew in the sanctuary, ushers still fanning her). Oh wine...why ya have to leave me honey! I luvs you...(sobbing)! I luvs you!

JC REPPA: (Frustrated) LIKE I WAS SAYIN'!...I want to say farewell to gang violence, drug use, and jail, *son!* May you all rest in peace! Now I lay my Glock down to sleep, I pray the Lord bury it deep...

PHAT JOHNNY: Mann...this dude reciting nursery rhymes?!

JC REPPA: (Continues rap) Sellin' drugs...you had to retire. Putting poison in my peep's blood gave me nightmares. I gotta step up and be the man God called me to be. How I'mma rep JC and my soul is filthy!

GRANDMA GOSPEL: PREACH BOY! You betta tell it! Tell it like it T-I-IS! (Yelling) TELL IT!!!

JC REPPA: (Bottle of grape juice in hand, pours a little on the ground) This is for my homies! (Pours juice again) This is for Pookie and 'nem. (Takes a sip from the bottle) This is for my Lord and Savior Jesus Christ; I do drink this in remembrance of Thee!

GRANDMA GOSPEL: (Snaps out of crying) We havin' communion? Nobody told me we was havin' communion?! Where the crackers at?...I ain't touchin' that grape juice...might make me relapse!

PHAT JOHNNY: Granny, you off the chain-n-n-n!...

GRANDMA GOSPEL: Ain't off the chain son, jus' off the booze! Jus' off the booze!

---

*The dialect of these characters are written phonetically to capture the true essence of Southern dialect and urban street slang.

God's Classifieds

HELP WANTED:

Missions: Great job with excellent benefits! Locations include food pantries, hospitals, nursing homes and homeless shelters. Various candidates needed nationwide! Soulfully and spiritually rewarding!
APPLY NOW: Team Jesus!

IMMEDIATELY NEEDED:

Ambassadors for Christ! Make a difference: spread the love of Jesus! Little experience? No problem! Start where you are: Co-workers, family, friends and neighbors are excellent candidates!

PUT YOUR SKILLS TO WORK!!!

Seeking PRAYER WARRIORS: people who will pray and intercede for the hurting, hungry, lost, and unsaved at least ONE HOUR A DAY! Those who don't know what a prayer closet is need not apply!

Life VS. Death

ANNOUNCER: Ladies and gentlemen, in this corner we have the undefeated champ: *LIFE!* In the far right corner we have none other than the life crushing, formidable opponent: *D-E-A-T-H-H!* It's going to be a tough fight, but the *"stronger"* in you, will come out on the winning side! You choose!

RELIGION doesn't cause war! Religion was built on the foundation of love! It is those who use religion for their own personal agenda that causes spiritual disharmony.

LIFE------> Sucka Punch!

POWER does not destroy a man. It's how he chooses to use his power. **Hitler** abused his power. **Mother Theresa** gave hers away.

DEATH------> Staggering in round two...

WORDS are God's gift of communication. People misuse words by speaking hate to cause hurt! It's a choice: words can be used to give life...or kill a spirit!

LIFE AND DEATH----> Are in a toe to toe match!

An evil man may kill the physical body with a gun, but the hole left in the soul from a bullet of hateful words, murders a life!

DEATH-----> Is backed up in the corner!!!

KNOWLEDGE is said to be power. It can be a deadly virus in the mind of a maniac, or a savior in the mind of a redemptive soul:

"I'm no longer a man of war, I died a man of peace."
-Stanley "Tookie" Williams III (Crips gang founder).

LIFE-----> The undisputed champion!!!

SOLDIER IN THE ARMY

Oh if I must be persecuted for righteousness sake, I'll walk through the valley of darkness, heart held high.

If I don't make it all the way out, count me among my great forefathers who lit my torch so I could carry on the fight; those who beat down hatred, racism, and cowardice with one word: **LOVE.**

Those whose lives were a sacrifice on God's altar. Those whose blood was shed because they fought for civil rights and freedom; let my fight be as courageous as theirs!

I say, let me compare my suffering as a gnat to a mountain compared to their throes on their battlefield.

Yet still my Lord, let my fight be as tenacious as a hungry lion capturing its prey!

With each wound I endure for the sake of freedom, let my voice scream loudly—reverberating a cry of spiritual awakening throughout the four corners of the earth!

Let my cry shut up evil's ears, blind terrorist's eyes, and mute the lips of war!

Let my warfare ignite an uprising of the Godhead, let it insight a mutiny of soldiers revolting for truth, morality, purity, and godliness!

Let me stand as courageous as David in the face of a modern day Goliath; leaving with the enemy's head held high as a sign of valor of spiritual defeat!

So war, I welcome you! I look proudly to that day that I will be robed with royalty, seated among the valiant of God's great army!

For I have nothing to lose in this life, but a lost soul, and Christ to gain.

It is God that girdeth me with strength, and maketh my way perfect. He maketh my feet like hinds' feet, and setteth me upon my high places. He teacheth my hands to war, so that a bow of steel is broken by mine arms. Psalm 18:32-3 (KJV).

Granny Gospel Wisdom

GRANNY GOSPEL: One is the loneliest number? Chile...not when you got Jesus!

Shootin' my Gospel guns atcha five times:

BOOM! If you always need people to validate you...your lips may be smiling, but your heart is weeping!

BOOM! If people weather your life to hide your loneliness, God will make the storms thunder louder to isolate you to Him!

BOOM! Getting full off of a worldly buffet results in spiritual starvation.

BOOM! If your life is cluttered with outer chaos, it means your internal house is not in order.

BOOM! If you have to have a lot of people around you all the time, quite simply...you don't like being alone with *YOU*!

---

*The dialect of this character is written phonetically to capture the true essence of the Southern dialect.

I am weak, yet *I Am Strong*

Beloved, from time to time you may look at your life from a vantage point of discouragement and disappointment. Dreams, goals, and plans that you had as a child have somehow become but a distant memory–lost somewhere in the cluttered closet of life; buried deep under a pile of mortgage payments, bills, work overload, family obligations and stress. You may suffer from a severe health problem, physical handicap, or have experienced a great loss in your life. You have given up on your passion, feel you are inadequate, or may think that your window of opportunity has not only closed, but slammed shut! Only if you can look past yourself to the One who is faithful! One who hears your prayers, and **The One** who give us hope! If you could only just believe, with God all things are possible (Mark 10:27)! The great news is, God is not a respecter of persons. All He tells us to do is just ask and believe! (Mark 11:24). If you would simply give your limitations to Him, He will do it in His strength, not yours! One of my favorite verses, **Zechariah 4:6, says not by might nor by power, but by my spirit,** says the Lord of Hosts. Where our natural reasoning stops, God's supernatural takes over!

Be encouraged beloved! If we examine God's character, He often uses the rejected, dejected, and outcasts of this world to perform great works in Him! It's not your abilities God chooses to use, but it's your disabilities that humbles you so that God can use you! The following are great, triumphant stories of broken wings that flew on the shoulders of triumph, perseverance, and determination!

The stone which the builders rejected has become the chief cornerstone.
Psalm 118:22

Vincent Van Gogh

Vincent Van Gogh, 20th Century painter of such works of art as: *At Eternity's Gate and The Starry Night,* is a legend in his own right. His paintings posthumously catapulted him to become one of the world's most revered *Dutch Impressionist* painters. It is estimated a Van Gogh Portrait, today, sells for up to $90 million dollars! AlthoughVan Gogh is considered a prodigy, his formative years would have predicted a very different ending. Van Gogh struggled with a life of depression, anxiety, and epileptic seizures, among a host of other life debilitating illnesses and phobias. As a precocious child, Van Gogh developed a passion for drawing. His depictions of nature and everyday life would only solidify his craft by the time he became a young adult. Having been professionally taught how to paint at Willem II College, not much later, Van Gogh sought out to become a professional artist. As an abecedarian, he struggled to sell his art work, and was often met with harsh criticism. Broke and destitute, he then decided to look for a more steady job.

After landing a short-lived job with an art dealer, Van Gogh started to develop a strong passion for religion and had a desire to "preach the gospel everywhere." Van Gogh then acquired another job working as a Methodist minister's assistant, and later traveled to Amsterdam to study Theology, but reportedly failed the entrance exam. It is said Van Gogh would spend much of his time translating passages from the Bible into English, German and French! In 1879, Van Gogh served as a missionary in a village in Belgium. He later returned back to Brussels to attend art school, and thus began the journey of one of the most prolific painters in history. The latter of Van Gogh's life in and around the art scene, coupled with his unfortunate battle with various sicknesses and diseases would produce a dichotomy of pain and brilliance in Van Gogh's work; paintings that were inspired by his love of realism, while vulnerably exposing the soul of a man marred by an onerous life. Because of a life of suffering, Van Gogh often felt like he was trapped inside of an inescapable black hole, and ironically, it was that same suffering that created his most beautiful form of expression–painting.

To Van Gogh, God and art were synonymous. He once stated:

"To try to understand the real significance of what the great artists, the serious masters, tell us in their masterpieces, that leads to God; one man wrote or told it in a book; another in a picture."

Thomas Edison

"I have not failed. I've just found 10,000 ways that won't work."
–Thomas Edison

In primary school, practically every child was taught a history lesson about the famous creator who invented the light bulb: Thomas Edison. Interestingly, most teachings about Edison's life only delve his accomplishments as an inventor, often excluding his early childhood life in which he struggled with learning disabilities and lost his hearing. At seven-years-old, Edison was said to have first attended school in Port Huron, Michigan. His primary teacher, the Reverend Engle, labeled him as hyperactive and maligned him as "stupid" because he was a curious child that asked a lot of questions. Moreover, Mr. Engle thought Edison was a slow learner and could not understand mathematics. As a child, Edison was also purported to have trouble paying attention, and he had a hard time speaking. More, Edison was mildly deaf in his left ear, and later would lose total hearing in that ear, and 80% of hearing in his right ear. Having been enrolled in school for only 3 months, Edison's mother Nancy, daughter of a Presbyterian minister, took him out of primary school and home schooled him. Nancy not only taught her son the fundamentals of academia, but also the Holy Bible. At age 11, Nancy introduced Edison to the local library where it is said that he had a great fondness for reading and read many books, his interest peaking in the area of science.

Because of his disabilities and hearing impairment, Edison did not return to secondary school, instead he worked odd jobs to support himself, while simultaneously working on his own experiments. Throughout the years, Edison would face extreme poverty. He got his lucky break when he was serendipitously hired by a brokerage firm in New York as a repair man! From there Edison's future began to change. An experiment he was working on, "*The stockticker,*" was his first marketable project that established his professional career as an inventor. A Corporation was so enamored with the invention that they paid him $40,000–an exorbitant amount of money in those days–for all of the rights to the device.

And thus began the career of the "Father of the electrical age," and retorted, "Greatest inventor who ever lived." As many learned in grade school, Edison was the inventor of the incandescent light bulb. But many do not know that he also invented over 1,093 patents. He is also credited as inventing the first silent film and also was the first person to blend audio with moving images! Now that's something I hadn't learned about him in school! And this all from a man who was stigmatized as having learning disabilities and who was considered legally deaf!

"Just because something doesn't do what you planned it to do doesn't mean it's useless." – Thomas Edison.

This biography by far inspires me the most! A person that literally did not obtain a formal education and pushed himself to succeed despite the bleak odds stacked against his life, is commendable! It should serve as a stark reminder that we were all born for a divine purpose and a plan by the creator God. As evidenced: handicaps, rejection and sickness may all be a part of that plan. Set backs are designed to set us up for greatness, to be better than average. It's pain that challenges us to work harder than others. It's pain that forces us to become better and excel higher! It's pain that causes mediocrity to escape us. If it were not for the battle, we would have never learned how to fight; we would have never learned how to defeat and conquer our enemies–both internal and external!

Ludwig Van Beethoven

Did you know that the, *"Christ on the Mount of Olives"* and *"Moonlight Sonata,"* composer and German pianist, Ludwig Beethoven, was deaf? Beethoven, known as one of the best–if not *the best*–musical composers and pianist of the 18th century, was not born deaf, but slowly succumbed to losing his hearing over the course of his lifetime.

It is documented that Beethoven suffered from a debilitating stomach illness that caused severe diarrhea and regurgitation that some doctors believed was a result of an auto-immune disease. At the age of 26, Beethoven began to experience a ringing sensation in his ears. Doctor's labeled it a severe form of tinnitus. The ringing in his ears was so bad that it was hard for him to hear music and engage in conversation. Almost completely deaf in the last ten years of Beethoven's life, he began to write books composed of letters to communicate back and forth with his friends. It is said that after his death, there were 400 conversation books of discussions between Beethoven and his friends. Although Beethoven began to lose his hearing, he was still writing, composing, conducting, and performing! Amazing!

A well documented story in the early 1800's, tells the heart-wrenching account of the ending of Beethoven's premiere of the *Ninth Symphony.* The audience was so enamored with the composition that it gave a roaring, standing ovation! Beethoven had to be turned around; hearing nothing, he wept. Beethoven eventually became completely deaf, which caused him great distress, bouts of depression and thoughts of suicide. Nonetheless, Beethoven's will to live was stronger than the thoughts of taking his life. He was continually inspired by music and art. At the advice of a doctor pending his deteriorating condition, Beethoven moved to the town of Heiligenstadt, not far from Vienna, in 1802 to rest from his condition. It was in this small Austrian town that Beethoven wrote his *Heiligenstadt Testament,* a letter to his brothers that records his struggle with his illness, but most importantly, it told of his resolve to continue living for his passion– the art of music!

"Don't only practice your art, but force your way into its secrets, for it and knowledge can raise men to the divine."
-Beethoven

Helen Keller

Helen Keller was a world renown author, speaker, and advocate; as well as an *American Foundation For The Blind* counselor. Helen Keller was left blind and deaf from an infection at the age of two. She lived a life of isolation: unable to speak words, unable to hear and was mute. She did not know what a word was until she would be taught by a specialist who worked with the blind and deaf, Annie Sullivan. Ms. Sullivan used a technique, a hand alphabet, which was signaled by touch. The device was placed in young Keller's hand during teaching sessions. It not only taught Helen how to spell, but later to read. As years passed, Helen became quite proficient in reading and writing. Keller would go on to write many books such as her autobiographies: *The story of my life, Light in my darkness,* and *Out of the dark*–to name a few. She became a sought after speaker and staunchly supported socialist issues. Helen Keller accomplished major achievements for a person who was both deaf and blind!

Helen Keller did not speak publicly about religion. Although she believed in God, it was reported she did not attend church. As a child, she was taught the *New Church doctrines of Emanuel Swedenborg.* The doctrine's teaching stated that the mission of Christianity was to make divine love a reality; a theology which paralleled with Helen's love of social causes. Keller would later befriend a preacher in the United States named Phillips Brooks. In a letter written to Bishop Brooks, Helen related that she had always known about God, even before she could formulate words. She said even before she had a name for God she knew He was there, but didn't quite know what it was. And even though she was in total darkness she knew she was not alone. She felt someone was with her. She said she felt God's love. So when she was taught language and heard about God, she said she already knew Him!

"I believe that through these dark and silent years, God has been using my life for a purpose I do not know. But one day I shall understand then I will be satisfied."

-Helen Keller

Fear not, for I am with you; Be not dismayed, for I am your God. I will strengthen you, Yes, I will help you, I will uphold you with My righteous right hand.

~Isaiah 41:10

Is Your Spiritual House Dirty?

When an unclean spirit goes out of a man, he goes through dry places, seeking rest, and finds none. Then he says, I will return to my house from which I came. And when he comes, he finds it empty, swept, and put in order. Then he goes and takes with him seven other spirits more wicked than himself, and they enter and dwell there; and the last state of that man is worse than the first. So shall it also be with this wicked generation. Matthew 12:43-45.

Has it taken a traumatic event in your life for God to open the window to your soul and show you a peek inside your spiritual house? Once inside, looking and searching around, you realize there is actually some dusting, cleaning, mopping, and washing to do! The chores seem overwhelming and you are in utter shock as your spiritual eyes have been opened to reality. You know that 1 *Corinthians 1:6,* says your body is a temple, yet you cannot understand how you let your house become so dirty! At this realization, you stop and kneel down on the floor of your heart and plead God's forgiveness; praying and asking Him to desperately change you. The dirt in your house could be bad habits, self-entitlement, arrogance, anger, vindictiveness, or low self-worth. Beloved, consider yourself blessed that you are even aware of your problem. Many people walk around in denial and pride, disastrously blinded by the offenses of their own behavior; whether the offense is against God or man.

If you truly desire to change, you will confess your sins, repent, and ask God to deliver you! So here comes the hard part: satan hears prayers too! He will try to do everything in his power to make you believe that you are a hopeless failure. He will begin to tell you that you will never change. He will put situations in your path that tests your willingness to change. Diabolically, he will begin to entice you with even stronger temptations when you are at your weakest point. Remember after Christ fasted forty days in the wilderness, and the devil came and tempted Him when He was most vulnerable? The devil is such a machiavellian, that he used the very doctrine that Christ preached against Him *(Matthew 4:1-11)* to try to persuade Jesus to follow him! So most certainly he will try to entice you to sin!

Here's the good news, Christ already defeated satan! He already won the victory for us on the cross—you just have to start believing it! The enemy will try to deceive you and convince you that your effort to change is in vain, but try not to get mad at yourself when you make a mistake, slip up, or relapse. Do you know it is purported to take *21-days* to break a habit? But with God it can take just one day! You have to keep going. God will deliver you in His timing, for His purpose and will. He may not deliver you right away because there are some things He wants you to learn. He will allow strongholds to mature you spiritually, prune, and sharpen you for His glory.

When you relapse it is just a reminder to keep working on that problem!

Your strongholds may be a struggle with the flesh, mental, emotional or personality problems, or character flaws. If you have lost all hope that your situation can change and it looks like there is no way out, let me give you the keys to unlock your prison doors:

<u>Reinvest in you</u> Get to the root of what is making you sad, depressed, or settling for less than what you deserve, and begin a journey to start loving yourself and putting *you* first. Start writing daily in a journal to monitor your thoughts and negative behavior patterns. If you're in a bad relationship, job, or dissatisfied with your life, change your environment. Don't settle for less! Determine what it is that you really want in life and go after it.

Read, study up on it, take classes then step out on faith and pursue it!

Make a commitment to change Stop compromising your good morals and values. Whether you're in an adulterous relationship, fornicating, lying, stealing, cheating or partying and drinking too much, you have to know that you're worthy of a better life! Just look back and see all the destruction this way of living has caused you and let that propel you to want to be a better person.

Commit to God You will not become free on your own will-power or in your own strength alone. Get serious with God and pour your heart out to Him. Even if you feel you have done too many bad things in your life, or you are waiting to clean yourself up first, why not let God do it? Just like the prodigal son, God is waiting with open arms to celebrate your return.

Seek help Don't suffer in silence. Solicit the help of a trained professional for your situation. Sometimes just opening up and confiding in a loved one or friend can help and encourage you. Far too many sufferers conceal their problems and let it emotionally destroy them. Don't let pent up anger and frustration rule your life. Get the help you need!

Deliverance Ministry Lastly, if you've done all you can and you still aren't making any progress, or some things you just can't seem to break free from, your problem may be of a demonic nature. I would suggest visiting a deliverance ministry and letting appointed men of God lay hands on and agree with you regarding stubborn sins, strongholds, or problems that won't subside (James 5:14). There are men and women anointed in the area of exorcism, casting out of demonic spirits, and breaking generational curses (More on this subject in chapter 35).

In the Old Testament, the temple was a sacred place where people went to worship God. Today, the temple is still sacred, but it is no longer a physical place, it is now located within our bodies. God lives in us! We must keep our temple holy and pure.

1 Corinthians 6:19

Or do you not know that your body is the temple of the Holy Spirit who is in you, whom you have from God, and you are not your own? For you were bought at a price; therefore glorify God in your body and in your spirit, which are God's.

God is calling you to get your spiritual house in order! Below are verses that will help you to start *soul* cleaning:

Psalm 51:10	1 Thessalonians 4:3-5	Isaiah 1:16-18
Psalm 51:7	Haggi 2:10-23	Ephesians 5:26
Matt 23:25-28	2 Corinthians 7:1	

In those days Hezekiah was sick and near death. And Isaiah the prophet, the son of Amoz, went to him and said to him, Thus says the Lord: Set your house in order, for you shall die and not live. In those days Hezekiah was sick and near death. And Isaiah the prophet, the son of Amoz, went to him and said to him, Thus says the Lord: Set your house in order, for you shall die and not live. Then Hezekiah turned his face toward the wall, and prayed to the Lord, and said, Remember now, O Lord, I pray, how I have walked before You in truth and with a loyal heart, and have done what is good in Your sight. And Hezekiah wept bitterly. And the word of the Lord came to Isaiah, saying, Go and tell Hezekiah, Thus says the Lord, the God of David your father: I have heard your prayer, I have seen your tears; surely I will add to your days fifteen years. Isaiah 38:1-5.

Natural Organic Mood Lifter

This is the day that the Lord has made, I will rejoice and be glad in it. Psalm 118:24

There are times when as soon as I awake, my mind is off and running what seems to be a marathon of duties, commitments and things that I have to do for the day, not to mention the concerns of yesterday. Sometimes I'm overwhelmed before my foot even hits the floor. To silence the murmur and chatter of the mind, *Psalm 118:24,* is one of the verses I like to recite before I even get out of bed in the morning. The day is surely going to be filled with its share of challenges, stressors, and oftentimes upsets. To combat negative mind chatter, I commit to memory and recite aloud *warfare* Bible verses and confess them over myself throughout the day! I am using the word as a sword to battle my spiritual enemies! Whatever your mind believes, your emotions and actions are sure to follow suit. For me, it's an instant picker-upper and mood booster! It's called **prophesying** over your life! You are using your mouth to pull down evil thoughts that are harassing your mind! Not only are you changing the chemistry of your thought patterns, but you are scattering darkness and speaking light into what you want to manifest in your life! Proverbs 18:21 says:

Death and life are in the power of the tongue, and those who love it will eat its fruits.

When the above verse is quoted, "*and those who love it will eat of its fruits,*" is often left out. When one thinks of fruit, he or she thinks of food, nutrition, health and something life sustaining—that is **speaking the word of God over your life**! It's your spiritual food! It does you no good to believe the Bible and not *confess* it! Eat it as your daily bread, it is your dose of life-sustaining manna! Words are invisible currents of energy that manifests life into what comes out of the mouth. As a Christian, it is imperative to discipline oneself in the mind/mouth connection. Diligently, you must use the mouth to always speak encouraging words, edification and exhortation. Not only towards yourself but others as well. More, the thought process operates at the speed of light and if you are not careful, you can find yourself meditating on a negative comment, mistakes you've made, or even the past. Before you know it, you have condemned yourself in your mind, only for it to manifest in the physical realm as your actions, and most often as your attitude. Beloved, lots of times you tell people a great deal about yourself, not only by what you say, but also by your behavior and your attitude! Your attitude is simply a release of your thoughts into physical form!

Learning to prophesy over your life is a *process*; it'll take time, perhaps years to fully grasp the concept of attacking negative thoughts as they arise. But a great place to start is beginning to monitor what you say to yourself, then ask, "Would I say this to someone else?" A great book of the Bible to meditate on and study is the book of James. It teaches a great deal on the mouth, its challenges, and how you should speak.

1-800-J-E-S-U-S

A Date With Destiny

Ladies! Are you constantly approached by men on the street calling you pet names and asking for your phone number? **Well...HAVE WE GOT A SOULTION FOR YOU!!!** (Details Below).

Man: Hello beautiful! Whassup Ma! Shorty! Boo! _____(fill in your blank!) Can I get your phone number so I can get to know you better?

Woman: (Megawatt smile) Sure: 1-800 J-E-S-U-S! Actually, He would like to get to know you better! To speak with him faster, please call His direct line: Matthew 6:9-13!

Man: (Dumbfounded) 1-800-Jesus? What?!

Woman: Yes! Please don't let this be a chance meeting, I would like to spend eternity with you! So please accept His call in Romans 10:9, and speak with God today!

A Friend That Sticks Closer Than A Brother

Co-worker: I have so many problems and I just don't have anyone to talk to!

Friend: Girl, I've got the perfect friend for you! His number is: 1-800-J-E-S-U-S!

Co-worker: 1-800-J-E-S-U-S #@!?

Friend: Girl, I once felt alone and afraid at one time in my life and I didn't have anyone to talk to, so I finally called *1-800-J-E-S-U-S!* I labored and was heavy laden, and He gave me rest **(Matt 11:28)**! You see, He was once tempted as we are, so He is able to sympathize with our weaknesses **(Hebrews 4:15)**. He encourages me, comforts me, and He shows me affection and sympathy **(Phillippians 2:1)**! He's a friend that sticks closer than a brother **(Proverbs 18:4),** and He loves at all times **(Proverbs 17:17)**! And you know what is so awesome? He calls me His friend too! **(John 15:15).**

Co-worker: Wow! You afraid? What's that number again?

Friend: 1-800-Jesus!

Co-worker: I'm gonna call as soon as I get home!

Friend: You don't have to wait until you get home, you can call Him right now! He's available 24/7 to answer your call!

John 3:16

For God so loved the world, that he gave his only begotten Son, that whosoever believeth in him should not perish, but have everlasting life.

A Doctor In The Courtroom

Man: I was in an accident! I'm hurt, out of work, my money's funny and I can't sleep! I need help!

Lawyer: Dial **1-800 J-E-S-U-S!** He's a doctor **(Jehova Rapha)**, a provider **(Jehova Jireh)**, a Justice of Peace **(Jehova Shalom)** and our Banner **(Jehovah Nissi).** He covers us, protects us and in Him we have victory!

For whoever calls on the name of the Lord shall be saved. Romans 10:13

The Devil Answers Prayers Too!

Ladies, so you are on a mission to do some much need inner work. You've taken meticulous notes at church, attended self-improvement classes, read books, attended seminars and practically ate, prayed and slept the Bible. You made some mistakes in the past and are determined to get it right this time. You've been badly hurt, and because of that big hole that's left in your heart, you're forced to give yourself time to heal. And while you're at it, you figure you can spruce yourself up a bit; get a new hairdo, join a gym and maybe lose a few pounds!

It took a few years but you put in the hard work and it has paid off! Your faith is renewed, your hope restored and your soul is at peace. There you are walking down the street head held high, hair blowing in the wind, with confidence as your stride! You are glowing! Your light is shining so brightly...you almost cause an accident! That tall, dark, and handsome man was so blinded by your glow that he slammed on breaks—nearly parking in the street—to jump out of his BMW just to talk to you! You, quite flattered, just couldn't stop blushing.

He approaches you very gentlemanly with such admiration and adorning words. *Ok, you got my attention,* you think to yourself. As he furthers along in his adulation, thoughts are running through your mind faster than a high-speed car chase! The young man tells you that he is a Christian and that he has been praying for a wife, and God told him that *you* are the one! You smile in agreement: this is your confirmation! *Thank you God! This is exactly what I have been praying for!* Heart palpitating, (in your mind) you exclaim: *Yes! God has finally sent me a husband!* Your attention is now perked higher than a Doberman Pension's ears! *Tell me more!*–your heart is faintly uttering. As Mr. tall, dark, and handsome continues, you notice him licking his lips. *Did he just lick his lips*? Now cautiously listening to his rhetoric, you notice his eyes are scanning your body like an X-ray machine at JFK airport. *Aah...hello...my face is up here!* You exclaim! *Um...did he just just do that?* RED FLAG! Ok...so you squeamishly still listen. He then proceeds to ask your name, you reluctantly tell him. For the sake of tact you ask his name. He replies Ishmael (the sound of a scratched record screeches loudly in your mind!) Momentarily frozen in your tracks, you then take off running faster than Usain Bolt running the men's 100 meters! Poor guy is left standing there, wondering what went wrong.

Beloved, this is a hilarious but true story of what happened to me one day as I was walking down a busy New York street. I couldn't help but laugh hysterically at its literalism. God does have a sense of humor! And after all, the Bible does say laughter is good for the soul! (Proverbs 17:22). But when life has taken you around the block a few times—humm...up and down the block and dragged you across the block too—you get to a place where you surrender every area of your life to God. You desire the heart of God and desire to be obedient to His word and His will for your life. The story of Abraham and Sarah greatly influenced me in my early Christian walk. I was very well versed in the book of Genesis. I was not about to settle for an Ishmael, when God had promised me an Issac! Of course this story does not speak on behalf of all persons named Ishmael, but figuratively in this instance. Even though this man was charming, incredibly attractive, and financially stable; because I am a diligent spiritual student, I knew he was not from God (Galatians 5:16).

The problem many people face is, they don't know who they are in Christ! They are not sensitive to that still, small voice, to hear what God tells them do. When you are not spending time with God in solitude is when you entertain the enemy's voice! I put in the time to get to know God; to learn His voice (John 16:13). Therefore, I knew the enemy when he showed up! How many of you have been so spiritually blinded that a wolf showed up in your life and you thought is was a sheep? (Matthew 7:15). Beloved if a person tries to change the essence of who you are, you may need to find out who answered your prayer! Maybe you are celibate and someone is trying to convince you sex is a natural, human behavior outside of marriage. Maybe you don't eat beef and a love interest is trying to tell you a million ways why beef is good. Or, maybe you have given your life totally to the Lord, and a romantic interest is trying to get you to go out to night clubs and drink alcohol, telling you there's nothing wrong with having a little fun and a few drinks. Or, perhaps he or she is trying to convince you to lie, steal, or cheat in certain areas of your life. The devil answers prayers too!

When you pray, the devil will sometimes send a replica; he sends an answer that looks exactly like what you have prayed for. But the Bible gives wise counsel:

Now I urge you, brethren, note those who cause divisions and offenses, contrary to the doctrine which you learned, and avoid them. For those who are such do not serve our Lord Jesus Christ, but their own belly, and by smooth words and flattering speech deceive the hearts of the simple. Romans 16:17, 18.

Beloved, the enemy knows God's plans for your life and he will try to do everything he can to get you to go down the wrong path. As Christians it is imperative to learn the teachings of the three voices.

There are three voices that speaks into your spirit:

1. **God's voice**
2. **Your voice**
3. **Satan's voice**

Many Christians struggle in this area of their walk. Many are often in utter confusion as to what voice is speaking into their spirit at any given time, or find it difficult to hear the voice of God. The Bible says:

My sheep hear my voice, and I know them, and they follow me (John 10:27 KJV).

Loved one, it's your right as a Christian to be able to discern the voice of the Father when he speaks to you! This is where spiritual warfare comes in to play. If you want to be an effective witness for Christ, you must learn how to pray *doctrinal prayers*. Doctrinal prayers are simply praying God's written word back to Him; reiterating His promises spoken in the Bible. Moreover, you must learn how to cover yourself when you go into the prayer closet. First, you have to get in the habit of asking for the assistance of the Holy Spirit (Romans 8:26). Then you must test the spirit by asking if it is indeed God's spirit, particularly if you are praying in tongues! God answers! You must also bind any spirit that is not a spirit of God and command it to leave your presence. Oftentimes this shows up as spirits of distraction, confusion, and disruption.

Prayer

Heavenly Father, I come to you in the name of your son Jesus Christ. I ask for the assistance of the Holy Spirit because the Bible says we know not what we should pray for as we ought, but the Spirit itself makes intercession for us with groaning which cannot be uttered. Father, I ask that you reveal yourself to me in this prayer hour. Let your voice be tangible to my spirit. Any spirit that is not the voice of God, I command you to leave my presence! In the name of Jesus I pray. Amen!

A great book that teaches on spiritual warfare is: ***Overcoming the Adversary,*** by Mark I. Bubeck. It also has a plethora of great spiritual warfare prayers pertaining to different areas of life. If you begin to pray in this fashion, diligently study the word of God, and incorporate fasting into your Christian walk, God's voice will start to become more clearer to you.

When you grow in your Christian walk your ears will become more sensitive to the spirit. You will gain spiritual discernment, and God will begin to reveal things to you in the spirit realm. Additionally, when God gives you a promise you have to stand still until you receive further instructions. Oftentimes we get a word from God and go ahead of Him in our flesh and try to make things happen, and that's when disaster happens. If we go back to the book of Genesis, remember the promise God gave to Abraham?:

After these things the word of the Lord came to Abram in a vision: "Fear not, Abram, I am your shield; your reward shall be very great." But Abram said, "O Lord God, what will you give me, for I continue childless, and the heir of my house is Eliezer of Damascus?" And Abram said, "Behold, you have given me no offspring, and a member of my household will be my heir." And behold, the word of the Lord came to him: "This man shall not be your heir; your very own son shall be your heir" (Genesis 15:1-4 ESV).

But we soon learn later in Genesis 16, that Sarah went ahead of God and gave her Egyptian handmaiden, Hagar, to her husband Abraham, thus Ishmael was conceived. God still blessed Ishmael's seed, but Sarah had to endure the consequences of Hagar's contempt.

The enemy wants to rob you of God's promises for your life: the career, spouse, ministry, children, peace, and joy that God has ordained specifically for you!

The thief does not come except to steal, and to kill, and to destroy. I have come that they may have life, and that they may have it more abundantly. John 10:10.

Beloved, the Bible also says:

Every good gift and every perfect gift is from above, and comes down from the Father of lights, with whom there is no variation or shadow of turning. James 1:17.

Make time for God to ensure it is He who answers your prayers!

The Game

God may let the devil get to the 1ˢᵗ, 2ⁿᵈ, or even 3ʳᵈ base in your life, but stay in the game, He's going to give *you* the home run!

When you are on Team Jesus, it may seem like the devil is playing football with your life: tackling you to the ground and kicking you around. You are going to get knocked down, hurt, and set back a few yards. But take it for the team, God's hand is always on the ball and He scores touchdowns!

Sometimes when you pray, it feels like you are playing a long game of golf. Your prayer may go over the hill and through the woods (pun intended), but eventually you will get the birdie!

You may have a baller that is a devil on the court of your life, but keep playing...watch how God is going to dribble on satan! Can you say, "Slam dunk?!"

Sometimes it may feel like you are drowning in the pool of life. You can barely keep your head above your problems. Keep swimming, each lap is your training ground; it's teaching you how to swim with the sharks!

I have fought the good fight of faith, I have finished the race, I have kept the faith. 2 Timothy 4:7. **But** *he who endures to the end will be saved. Matthew 24:13.*

I Gave Up Religion And Went Back To Drinking

Let's face it, it seems as if stress and tiredness are lurking around every corner of our lives. If it isn't pressure on the job or friction within our relationships, it's worry over bills, finances and money. Beloved, the times are definitely getting harder, and the days more and more demanding. It's a synonymous feeling of heaviness reverberating throughout the spiritual realm. One of the biggest challenges facing mankind today is managing time. There's work, children, meeting your spouse's needs, home duties, church commitments—to say the least. Oftentimes during the course of a week, this may leave one frazzled, beat, and feeling s-t-r-e-t-c-h-e-d out! Oh, did I also mention packing on the pounds; because yeah, stress makes us eat! "When will it ever end?" You may ask yourself. "How will I ever find an oasis in this dry desert of my life?" (Ezekiel 19:13,14).

If you are constantly busy with life's affairs, you have to be careful not to neglect your prayer life and time spent with God. Many people relegate time spent with God to church on Sunday; where they are serving on *this* board, serving in *that* ministry, and not to mention feeding the homeless after church. You're working for the Lord, and surely you will be blessed for serving in His kingdom—you tell yourself. Although, in your heart you can't understand why you *aren't* being blessed because you are such a good person and you do so much good for others. So, there you go off to church yet another Sunday, at the altar—yet again—asking *sister* *"SavedsanctifiedandHolyGhostfilled,"* to keep you lifted up in prayer.

On Communion Sunday, you partake of The Lord's Supper by raising your bread and cup and consuming your offerings, while not fully comprehending what it truly means! If we take a moment and go back and revisit 1 Corinthians 11:25, it admonishes: **In the same way also he took the cup, after supper, saying, "This cup is the new covenant in my blood. Do this, as often as you drink it, in remembrance of me."** It states, because of His shed blood for us, we, who accepted Him as our Savior, were put in a covenant relationship with Christ. If we define covenant, it means: **to be in agreement between two people.** He tells us that as often as we drink from this physical "cup" during communion, we are to remember that He died on the cross for our sins. When Christ died on the cross, His physical body left this earth, but He is still with us in spirit. If we delve this passage from a figurative perspective; Christ is admonishing us to drink from His spiritual cup, which is Living Water, in which He says we will never thirst again (John 4:14).

Beloved, there's certainly nothing wrong with serving in church, volunteering, or asking for prayer, but the problem is, it will only fill your spirit for so long. You have to go directly to the source for lasting fulfillment. You have to go to Christ and establish a one-on-one relationship with Him. He's waiting for you to come to Him. Good works alone won't save your soul. God prays for you! He prays on your behalf to the Father. In Luke 22:31-32, Jesus tells Simon that satan wanted to sift him as wheat, but He prayed for him. Also, in John 14:16-17,

Christ told the disciples that He will pray for them and ask God to send them another helper: the Holy Spirit. Christ helps us by petitioning our requests to God when we go to Him in prayer! Hallelujah! It is imperative that you establish a personal relationship with Christ and spend time with Him daily; praying and diligently studying the word yourself, not depending on your pastor. Beloved, the times are becoming increasingly evil. It is of utmost importance that saints get serious about the kingdom of God! You must train yourself to seek God *first* when serious problems arise in your life. God forbid, there may come a time when you may not have access to a physical Bible. As the Psalmist says in Psalm 119:11, **"Your word I have hidden in my heart that I might not sin against you."** Saints, you need to know how to reach God in times of distress and in times of temptation to fight your own battles.

Moreover, when you make a habit of spending time with God, you will break the chains of bondage off areas of your life that are troubling you! Not that your life will become any easier, but God will give you the provision and peace to face any situation that you will go through in your life! Hallelujah! It is a peace unlike anything you have ever experienced before. It is a sacrifice, and will be challenging time wise to make commitments to spend with God, but the rewards are everlasting! Beloved, God will begin to fight your battles supernaturally (Exodus 14:14). You will notice things will not easily bother or upset you the way they used to. I guarantee God will give you a new vision to see problems differently in your life. Most importantly, He will walk beside you, holding your hand as you go through each trial. So the next time you find yourself at a deep well like the Samaritan woman, drink from the source of the river of Living Waters: Jesus Christ.

A woman from Samaria came to draw water. Jesus said to her, "Give me a drink." 8. (For his disciples had gone away into the city to buy food.) 9. The Samaritan woman said to him, "How is it that you, a Jew, ask for a drink from me, a woman of Samaria?" (For Jews have no dealings with Samaritans.) 10. Jesus answered her, "If you knew the gift of God, and who it is that is saying to you, 'Give me a drink,' you would have asked him, and he would have given you living water." 11 The woman said to him, "Sir, you have nothing to draw water with, and the well is deep. Where do you get that living water? 12 Are you greater than our father Jacob? He gave us the well and drank from it himself, as did his sons and his livestock." 13. Jesus said to her, "Everyone who drinks of this water will be thirsty again, 14. but whoever drinks of the water that I will give him will never be thirsty again. The water that I will give him will become in him a spring of water welling up to eternal life." 15. The woman said to him, "Sir, give me this water, so that I will not be thirsty or have to come here to draw water."

John 4:7-15

When your spirit is thirsty, drink from the everlasting fountain of life–*JESUS!*

Healing Balm Cafe:
Is your food making your sick?

AGAPE LOVE: Man shall not live by bread alone, but by every word the proceeds out of the mouth of God. As you ponder your spiritual health, are you eating wholesome manna that is life sustaining and life giving, or are you dying a slow death...feasting on the junk food of the soul: seeds of worry, fruit of doubt, and the bread of despair and hopelessness?

PHAT JOHNNY: Granny, you hear dat? That junk food that you're eating is destroying your body! I command you in the name of Jesus, to take that Twinkie out of your purse right now!

GRANDMA GOSPEL: (Gives Phat Johnny the side eye).

JC REPPA: Phat Johnny...looks like you're the one that's eating all the Twinkies, Pillsbury "dough" boy!

*The dialect of these characters are written phonetically to capture the true essence of Southern dialect and urban street slang.

GRANDMA GOSPEL: Yeah, you right...that bread does make me constipated!

JC REPPA: She's talking about spiritual food, not real bread!

GRANDMA GOSPEL: (Quips)I know what bread she's talking about! That spiritual bread makes me constipated too! Nah...I can't do it!...my Bingo gets stopped up, my wine don't flow, and my boyfriend can't...

JC REPPA and PHAT JOHNNY: GRANNY!!!

GRANDMA GOSPEL: What?! I was gone say he can't come to my house no mo'! Don't want to tempt myself. I'm a Holy woman! Um hum...I'm stayin' pure till I get married (coughs)...again.

PHAT JOHNNY: AGAIN!...woman at the well, you been married 5 times already!

GRANDMA GOSPEL: That's it! You gone make me lose my religion! That's it! (Grabs her purse and Bible...runs after Phat Johnny).

PHAT JOHNNY: (Runs).

JC REPPA: Man...you runnin' from an old lady?!

GRANDMA GOSPEL: Yea he runnin' alright...runnin' out of breath!

PHAT JOHNNY: (Stops...bends over...hyperventilating like he's having an asthma attack).

GRANDMA GOSPEL: (Starts beating him over the head with her Bible!)

It's Not A Person Harassing You...

It's a spirit!

They came to the other side of the sea, to the country of the Gerasenes. And when Jesus had stepped out of the boat, immediately there met him out of the tombs a man with an unclean spirit. He lived among the tombs. And no one could bind him anymore, not even with a chain, for he had often been bound with shackles and chains, but he wrenched the chains apart, and he broke the shackles in pieces. No one had the strength to subdue him. Night and day among the tombs and on the mountains he was always crying out and cutting himself with stones. And when he saw Jesus from afar, he ran and fell down before him. And crying out with a loud voice, he said, "What have you to do with me, Jesus, Son of the Most High God? I adjure you by God, do not torment me." For he was saying to him, "Come out of the man, you unclean spirit!" And Jesus asked him, "What is your name?" He replied, "My name is Legion, for we are many." Mark 5:1-9 (ESV).

In Christianity, much of today's teaching focuses on prosperity Gospel, motivational preaching, Biblical history and the works of Biblical scholars. However, when the the topics of demons, demonic oppression or demonic harassment are raised, it is often delegated to antiquated Biblical rhetoric by some, spiritualism, or the opening of Pandora's box to others. Some pastors may teach in the area of spiritual warfare, but at surface level with no real introspection into the workings of the spirit world. Those afflicted by demonic oppression are often simply told to just "pray or fast the problem away," and are left tormented, isolated and suffer in silence. Some Christians don't even acknowledge its existence, choosing not to believe in the realization that there are different spiritual planes between heaven and earth. More, some religions even teach that there isn't a hell. Those who teach in the area of demonic warfare may be labeled zealots or extreme. God calls different people to different areas of ministry. I have read many books by several different pastors whom God have called into the ministry of *Deliverance*. More so known as exorcism, or subtly: the casting out of demons and demonic spirits. God gives us many examples in the Bible regarding demonic oppression and casting out wicked spirits. Yet those examples may seem superfluous to those who are not called to this ministry, the inexperienced or uninformed. In today's time, countless people are experiencing the same influences of demonic harassment or possession as told in the Bible! There are numerous testimonies recorded in documentaries, books, online, and in publications detailing the lives of men and women who have come face-to-face with demons: whether by influence, possession, victimization, the laying on of hands, casting out of wicked spirits, or deliverance from demons.

Have you ever ridden on a train or a bus perhaps, and you noticed a person sitting across from you that appeared to be talking to him or herself? You looked around hoping the person was talking to someone else, but you quickly realize it was a singular conversation. So quietly, you sat there listening in shock to the extent of the dialogue—between the person and him or herself—wondering if this is really happening or if you are the crazy one! This is a demonic strong hold! When people are born into this world they do not speak to themselves in this way! Over the years there was a constant attack sieged against their minds that was authored by satan himself! Unfortunately, many have lost this mental battle to the devil by way of paranoia, schizophrenia, Bi-polar disorder, phobias and the like. Let me clarify that not all of these illnesses are demonic in nature, but a vast majority of them are! Demonic warfare is very much real!

By far those are extreme cases of spiritual warfare. There are different levels of demonic influence and manipulation. What I want to talk to you about in this text is demonic influence on a more personal level, with people you encounter on a day-to-day basis: your family, friends, co-workers or casual encounters. When many think of spiritual warfare, what may come to mind is interceding in prayer for a specific situation, problem or person. But many often neglect to realize the spirit that is operating behind the scenes, which may go unnoticed to the spiritually undiscerned.

Paul says in Ephesians:

For our struggle is not against flesh and blood, but against the rulers, against the authorities,

against the powers of this dark world and against the spiritual forces of evil in the heavenly realms (Ephesians 6:12).

When we come into contact with unruly people or have bitter disagreements or altercations with people in our lives, our first reaction is to blame the other person, or resent them. If you allow bitterness or unforgiveness to overcome you, you haven't yet acknowledged or come to an understanding of the spirit the person is operating under. Beloved when you can grasp hold of this teaching, you will have better knowledge of the operation of the spirit realm. For the most part, your conjecture will change through prayer, study and reading; and over time with much trial-and-error training.

Be sober, be vigilant; because your adversary the devil walks about like a roaring lion, seeking whom he may devour (1 Peter 5:8 NKJV).

If we define vigilant, it is stated: "To be keenly watchful to detect danger." As well, sober in this context is not referring to being sober from alcohol, but being spiritually sober, meaning guarding your spirit man; keeping it healthy and pure, untainted from the lusts of the world. I have established the fact that spirits operating in the kingdom of darkness do tempt, manipulate and harass people. Christians are no exception! At any given time a Christian can be influenced by demonic spirits and may not even be aware or, are in denial. How so you say? Have you ever said or did something to someone and later wondered why did you say or do that? Has uncontrollable anger ever come over you as you were dealing with a customer service person or telemarketer, have you ever had a bad thought out of nowhere, used profane language, disliked a person for no reason, are moody, fantasize, have sexually immoral thoughts, given to gossip, have road rage, are self-loathing, or harbor unforgiveness?

Those are but a few examples of influences of the devil! The difference is, mature Christians will realize their transgression, repent and ask God to help them. Beloved, being a Christian doesn't exempt you from making human mistakes! If a person has not been trained in spiritual warfare, sadly, they may not even realize that they are being used by the devil. They may very well be claiming the title of a Christian, but are constantly defeated mentally and emotionally because of a lack of study in the area of demonic oppression.

Moreover, some people may unknowingly invite demonic oppression into their lives by living recklessly or living in willful sin. Thus, opening the door of their spirit to be influenced by the enemy. But the good news is, you have the power to drive demons out of your life!

Below are steps on how to break free from torment by the devil:

1. Live a godly life.

2. Establish a consistent prayer life outside of church services. Ask God to give you the gift of speaking in tongues if you don't already have it.

3. Find a good deliverance church.

4. Join a prayer group or prayer line dealing with spiritual torment or harassment.

5. Read and study books dealing with spiritual warfare, demonic oppression.

6. Establish a weekly fast.

7. Refrain from watching movies/TV shows/games involving horror, the occult, vampires, witches, and demonic activity.

8. Rid your home of any demonic artifacts, idols, statues, skulls and bones paraphernalia, things relating to darkness and death.

9. Stop the practice of visiting fortune tellers, tarot card readers, mediums and spiritualists.

10. Don't give up! Keep fighting for your deliverance!

And he ordained twelve...to have power to heal sicknesses, and to cast out devils. Mark 3:14-15 (KJV)

Who's Tied To Your Soul?

Many people have dated different partners over the course of their lifetime. Some even proudly proclaim that they have a *type!* This statement is truer than they actually realize! While many people speak of having a *physical* type, they also have a spiritual type! Unwittingly, many people keep choosing different partners but the same spirit! Those in dysfunctional or unhealthy relationships cannot understand why they keep ending up with the same kind of person. The answer lies partly in their spirit identifying with the other person's spirit (meaning that both people are operating on the same spiritual frequency). Say for instance a person is passive, but he or she keeps attracting an aggressive, controlling person. It means that the spirit that is operating in him or her at their current spiritual level is seeking to connect with its mirror reflection, whether good or bad. If a passive person is attracting an extreme opposite, it means that he or she is attracting an equally broken spirit: a person that is aggressive. His spirit is trying to fill a void, trying to fulfill something that he does not possess within himself, vice versa. He is subconsciously trying to make himself whole, fulfilled, and complete. Thus, he or she keeps ending up with the same type of person trying to find happiness, wholeness; but only God can make one whole!

Sadly, many in this vicious cycle often mistake sex for love, and think sex is what will keep a person in their life. The spiritual connection is sealed when the relationship is consummated. When you have a sexual relationship with another person, you feel a strong attachment to them because your souls have been joined to each other. Even though you may have broken up with the person, if you have not prayed over your connection to them, you have not broken up with the spirit that is operating in them! Thus, every man or woman you date thereafter will be a different physical body, but the same spirit following you through each relationship.

That's why the Bible puts such emphasis on fornication, immorality and adultery. We were not created to have sex outside of marriage. The woman was created physically from a man's rib (Genesis 2:22), therefore there is a sacred connection between a man and a wife. The Bible says when a man and woman marry, they will become "one flesh" because their souls have become conjoined. When people fornicate, this broken covenant is the result of sexual disease, out of wedlock pregnancy, the break down of the family structure, and emotional discord between the male and female because of rebellion against God's word.

"But at the beginning of creation God 'made them male and female.' 'For this reason a man will leave his father and mother and be united to his wife, and the two will become one flesh.' So they are no longer two, but one flesh. Therefore what God has joined together, let no one separate" (Mark 10:6-9).

Moreover, when you commit adultery, you are not only physically sleeping with some one's husband/wife, but you are also copulating with the spirit of cheating, the spirit of lying, and the spirit of dishonesty! Therefore, you have made an agreement in the spirit realm with whatever characteristics this person has in his or her spirit. If we define copulating, it means: "connected or joined." Therefore beloved, you have "connected" the spirits to your soul. Those spirits are now a part of who you are! You made an agreement with them when you opened the door to sin. Because of submission to sin in one area of your life, you will be given to lying, cheating and dishonesty in other areas of your life. You have heard many a wives or husbands of cheating spouses utter, **"He or she has changed, she's not the same person as she was when we first got married, I feel like I don't even know him anymore!"** The cheating spouse will result to telling lie after lie, and manipulating scheme after scheme to cover his or her tracks. They will begin to operate out of character because they are under demonic subjection. In other words, their soul is being ruled by these spirits.

In continuation, abused women often find themselves selecting the same mate over and over again because they have entered into a soul agreement with an abusive, violent, controlling or manipulative spirit. Oftentimes, these soul ties are made before a woman is even born; by her parents. In most cases the mother has married an abusive or controlling man, and the spirit has been passed down her lineage to her daughter. A lot of women feel guilty because they cannot understand why they keep choosing the same type of man, but in actuality this spirit is the one that's pursuing them! If women are not aware of a controlling and abusive pattern they will keep entering into these same types of relationships. A woman has to begin to make a conscious effort to pay attention to the type of behavior patterns a potential male suitor exhibits.

Unfortunately, many women will deem this behavior acceptable because that's the example they were shown by their father or male figures growing up in the home. Many women marry replicas of their fathers. And many men marry women with their mother's characteristics. Most importantly, an abused woman must do a lot of spiritual work to break this generational curse and sever ties with this type of spirit. She must work on her self-esteem, self-worth, and learn to love and forgive herself; whether it's through church counseling, Bible study, or a self-help group. An abused woman must do some soul-searching to ascertain what causes her to make the choices that she makes; she must get to the root cause of her behavior, she must deal with childhood emotional wounds. She must forgive so she can heal herself! People carry two bags in life: childhood and generational. Abuse endured as a child is carried into adulthood, and each painful experience along the way is added to your life's bags. Generational curses are passed down from your lineage. Until you learn how to absolve it, you have no control over it, but God does! Let forgiveness heal your wounds so you can drop off inherited curses at God's door.

In my research and counseling, I have encountered many people who have been sexually abused or molested. Often I find that many take on the spirit of the molester by later becoming an abuser themselves. Others delve into pornography and illicit sexual behavior, and some who have been molested by a same-sex abuser, often enter into a soul tie with a homosexual spirit. It is called a spirit of transference. In no way am I saying all homosexuals are a result of a spirit of transference, but a majority of those whom I have personally spoken to; this has been their testimony. An abused person must do extensive soul searching and Biblical study to identify his or her true identity–that which God created you to be–to deflect the identity which has been opposed upon you by outside influences or the devil.

Additionally, a good majority of women who have been molested often turn to prostitution, drug use or promiscuous behavior. They enter into soul ties with spirits of self-hate, low self-esteem and low self-worth, hatred towards men, or self-harming behavior. There have been countless cases of gay, abused and lost men and women who have, through years of earnestly searching for their truth, found their true identity in Christ and have broken these soul ties off of their lives. But it is not easy! The devil will fight you every step of the way! But know beloved, it is your birth right to be spiritually free because Jesus Christ died on the cross for you!

In conclusion, breaking free from soul ties is attainable! Don't think for one moment you have to stay where you are: in a hopeless, dark and lonely place where it seems like you cannot escape a burdening sin or a demonic stronghold! God is a rescuer! It will take a strong desire and a willingness to want to change, and submitting to God's will for your life. I am living proof of how God can come in and put the pieces of a broken life back together again and use it for His kingdom! Amen! You must be very careful in guarding your spirit and what you open your spirit up to. That includes the people in your life; whether family, friends, or co-workers who influence you to engage in unscrupulous behavior, to staying away from establishments which activities may entice you to sin or situations that may cause you to compromise your spirituality or moral character.

Your Garden Of Gethsemane

Then Jesus came with them to a place called Gethsemane, and said to the disciples, "Sit here while I go and pray over there." And He took with Him Peter and the two sons of Zebedee, and He began to be sorrowful and deeply distressed. Then He said to them, "My soul is exceedingly sorrowful, even to death. Stay here and watch with me." He went a little farther and fell on His face, and prayed, saying, "O My Father, if it is possible, let this cup pass from me; nevertheless, not as I will, but as You will." Then He came to the disciples and found them sleeping, and said to Peter, "what could you not watch with me one hour? "Watch and pray, lest you enter into temptation. The spirit indeed is willing but the flesh is weak." Again, a second time, He went away and prayed, saying, "O My Father, if this cup cannot pass away from Me unless I drink it, Your will be done." And He came and found them asleep again, for their eyes were heavy. So He left them, went away again, and prayed the third time, saying the same words. Then He came to the disciples and said to them, "Are you still sleeping and resting? Behold, the hour is at hand, and the Son of Man is being betrayed into the hands of sinners." Matthew 26-45.

I love springtime! Living in the North, the anticipation of spring approaching every year excites me as I think about the warm weather, glowing sun, blue skies, and flowers in bloom; emitting fresh, sweet fragrances into the air! The nostalgia takes me back to my childhood; reminding me of the garden my sister and I used to play in in our back yard. As a child, perhaps you had a garden that you embraced, whether real or a figurative. A place where you found solace and comfort, a place where you could slip away from life and ponder your thoughts; a garden where you perhaps, found God. As the years have passed and life has taken its course, you now find that when you go into your secret garden, there are no sweet melodies from chirping birds, no fluttering butterflies, and the sun is now tucked away behind dark clouds. Maybe you have now found that the flowers have all wilted, binding weeds have sprung up, and what was once a place full of life, now feels cold, desolate and isolated. An overwhelming since of despair has arisen, and your soul feels like it's being swallowed up by the darkness that is surrounding you. You cry out in your heart, "Father, help me! Surely, you see my pain?!" Yet, the garden remains silent. Your cries seem to go unheard, pleas unanswered.

I can only imagine this is what Jesus must have felt on that day in the garden of Gethsemane. He knew His life was to be sacrificed, but at that very hour the reality of it all had become very immediate. Jesus knew that His Father had indeed allowed Him to go through that period of suffering in order to save many souls. Jesus knew that His death was a sacrifice so that His spirit could live on inside of us. Isaiah 61:1-3, says it best when the prophet says that the spirit of the Lord has come "...To give unto them beauty for ashes."

The prophet James admonishes us to, **"Count it all joy**

when you fall into various trials, knowing that the testing of your faith produces patience (James 1:1-3)."** I believe verse 4 really speaks the heart of James: **"But let patience have its perfect work, that you may be perfect and complete, lacking nothing."** As a babe in Christ, the book of James was one of my greatest encouragers. It would be very encouraging to say that as a Christian your life will be easy, all of your problems will dissipate or you won't have stormy seasons. But beloved, that is the farthest from the truth! While the Apostle Paul tells us that when we come to God we are saved by His grace, he also mentions, "For we who live are always delivered to death for Jesus' sake, that the life of Jesus may also be manifested in our mortal flesh (2 Cor 4:11)."

Even though you may be pious, you are going to go through periods of testing in your spiritual life. But be encouraged, Psalm 34:19 says, **"Many are the afflictions of the righteous, But the Lord delivers him out of them all."** Whatever trying situation you go through, you can take confidence in knowing that God always makes a way of escape. If you are at an impasse in your Christian walk, the following may be areas in your life that God is working on:

God is teaching you to worship Him

Has God not answered a prayer that you have been praying for years, and you're finding it hard to have faith because you just cannot understand why He hasn't intervened in this situation? You have been suffering for years, pleading with God to answer *this* prayer, yet it goes unanswered. You've given up and lost hope and find it hard to even pray about it anymore. You are *tired*! But the question is, in the midst of the trial are you thanking God? Are you praising Him? You're believing the enemy's lies that you aren't going to defeat this situation. You've given up hope. You've given up emotionally, therefore you're already defeated! If you can just have a mustard seed of faith and open up your mouth and start praising God, despite your situation, He will fight your battles! 2 Chronicles 20:15-25, tells the story of the people of Judah who would soon learn that they were going to be attacked by the Ammonites, Moabites and Menuites. Jehoshaphat, King of Judah, sought the Lord and proclaimed a fast throughout Judah. God answered the people of Judah:

Thus says the Lord to you, 'Do not be afraid and do not be dismayed at this great horde, for the battle is not yours but God's.'

2 Chronicles 20:15

Beloved, they didn't win the battle until they started *praising* God! The battle is not yours, it's the Lord's!

And when they began to to sing and praise, the Lord set an ambush against the men of Ammon, Moab, and Mount Seir, who had come against Judah, so they were routed.

2 Chronicles 20-22

God is teaching you to step out on faith and start worshipping and praising Him in the midst of your trials. Your worship determines your victory!

Has God called you to serve in ministry?

The word "bond" is defined as something that binds, confines, and unites. The Greek word for "servant" is *idoulos*; in the English language it means "Bond Servant." In doctrinal teaching bondservants weren't mere slaves, they were entrusted with their master's affairs. The Apostle James introduces himself as a "bondservant of God" in his letter to the 12 Tribes of Israel. To be a bondservant then, one must give up the will for his/her life and faithfully follow Christ. In Matthew 20:25-28, Jesus' life on this earth perfectly exemplified the heart of a servant. In verse 28, Jesus states, **"Just as the Son of Man did not come to be served, but to serve, and to give his life as a ransom for many."** A a Christian that should be the very call of your life.

There were several apostles in the Bible who proclaimed to be bondservants of Christ: Peter, Paul, Titus, as well as Jude (to name a few). Could it very well be that God is calling you to be a voice for this generation? Has God anointed you and is calling you into the ministry? In the Bible God spoke directly to His most cherished prophets, but after His Son was sent to die on the cross for us, He put The Holy Spirit within us so that we might all have a living relationship with Him. The Holy Spirit speaks intimately through the Bible, through the prompting of the spirit, through confirmations, and supernaturally reveals Himself to the servant who humbles himself before God. Beloved you have to earnestly seek God by shutting out the noise of the world in order to hear His voice. You have to go to your secret garden and plead with Him. Sometimes when you go through a spiritual battle it may feel like God isn't there. You may have cried out, **"God why aren't you helping me?"** Beloved, I feel like God is sitting on the sidelines, arms folded with confidence in his child and a smile on his face saying, **"You can do it! I have faith in you! I have equipped you with whatever you need to overcome!"** He is your biggest cheerleader!

Sometimes God has to allow you to go through difficult situations so you can experience, personally, His Sovereignty and faithfulness. Always remember, if you are earnestly seeking God you will always win the battle! You may have to suffer emotionally, physically, or financially at times, but God will give you peace either in the midst of the garden or after you come out of it. He will give you deeper wisdom and greater insight into the situation you are going through. After the storm, He pats you on the back saying, **"Job well done, you made it through! I knew you could do it!"** In my neophyte years as a Christian, I felt as if God were saying, "I allowed this battle so you will learn how to be a conqueror." In the end of each trial, I gave all the glory to Christ! (1 peter 1:6).

If God always came to your rescue, not allowing you to go through any hardships or trials, it would stunt your spiritual growth. Concluding, the road you travel on your Christian journey is preparing you for your appointed ministry in Him.

Is it persecution or spiritual maturing?

If you feel like everything in your life is falling apart, this testing is teaching you how to endure. It's calling you to a higher level of faith in God. It is teaching you how to suffer long, and most importantly, it's sharpening your understanding in the working of the spirit world. James 1:4, says **"But let patience have her perfect work, that ye may be perfect and complete, lacking nothing" (KJV).** If you open your mind to learning spiritual principles, you will realize that God *is* life's teacher! When you keep going through the same problem over and over, it is because you have not yet learned the lesson and grew from it. The operative word is *grow*. It's one thing to go through something and not learn the lesson; but it's another thing when you are still in bondage to it. The victory is won when you **learn** from it, **heal** from it, and **release** it–be freed from it! Hence, not only break through, but break free from the problem! If you fail to learn from any life experience, it will surely come back in different parameters in your life. For me it was forgiveness. God kept allowing people and situations in my life that required me to forgive. At the time I didn't understand it as such. My limited vision could only see the circumstance with physical eyes, *Lord, this person did this to me, did that to me...you have to deal with them Lord! Change them!* When quite simply the Lord was saying, **"No, I need to change you!"** Sometimes we need to take the log out of our own eye before we look at the log in our brother's eye (Matt 7:5). You have to learn how to look at every situation in your life from a spiritual perspective. When going through difficult times, your prayer to God should always be:

1. Teach me the lesson in this situation.

2. Give me the strength to endure.

3. Is there a character trait that you are trying to perfect in me?

4. Give me the patience and peace needed to go through this.

5. Give me wisdom and understanding. Unlock the limited areas in my thinking. Open my mind to what I'm not seeing.

6. Lord, give me the ability to love this person, and/or be at peace with him/her during this trying time.

7. Lord, give me the ability to forgive.

8. Remove the situation or give me the strength to go through it.

9. Help me to accept your will regarding this situation.

10. Help me to have faith in you and trust you.

You'd be amazed how may people don't ask God for what they want because they don't believe that they will get it. John 16:24, says ask so that your joy may be made full! More, when you pray, you have to have patience and trust God's timing. Sometimes God will allow you to go through difficult situations to teach you to focus on Him and *not* the problem. Also He may be working on your character before He can advance you.

1 Peter 1:7 says,

That the genuineness of your faith, being more precious than gold that perishes, though it is tested by fire, may be found to praise, honor, and glory at the revelation of Jesus Christ.

Of course it is not easy when you are being tested, but the above verse states that the resulting fruit that the trial produces in your life is what will give glory and honor to God! The darkness will fade, the flowers will bloom again, the grass will sprout, and you will have a newfound praise in your heart! You will have gone to the depths of where God lives and now know him more intimately! Hallelujah! God loves you, be encouraged!

Your Worst Enemy

It's six o' clock am. As you lay sleeping, the jarring alarm jolts your brain awake, while your body is still trying to hold on to the last few minutes of sleep. You jump up disoriented, heart racing, and dazed. You then dash out of bed to shower before stumbling over piles of clothes strewn all over the floor. Little Johnny starts screaming at the top of his lungs. *Where is that baby sitter?! She's usually here by...*before you can complete the sentence the phone rings and you hear a quaint voice on the other end of the line, "Hello...ugh...Hi Ms. Outtaorder, I'm not going to be able to come in today, something came up!" Seething, you quip, *The nerve of that little wench! She's supposed to be here already!; a*s you slam the phone down! You quickly sprint to the shower, after emerging, rummage through the accumulated junk compiled in your room that hasn't been cleaned in two weeks and find your phone book nestled underneath a plate of half-eaten, moldy Chinese food that exposed the deathly odor you had been trying to pin point.

You scramble through the phone book leaving messages out of desperation to every relative, church member, ex-boyfriend, ex-boyfriend's girlfriend trying to find a replacement sitter. "If you come to work late one more time, it will result in your termination!"; your cantankerous boss' voice resonates in the back of your mind. After leaving a barrage of voice messages as a result of unanswered phone calls, you hang up the phone in despair; hair dripping wet, car keys in hand, and little Johnny straddled across your hip. Tears start to stream down your face as scenes of a crumbling life play out in your mind's eye. You plop down on the bed and begin to question God: **Lord, my life is a mess! My husband left me, I don't know how I'm going to pay the mortgage this month, and how am I going to raise this child that you have given me? Lord, I don't understand...I walked away from the world and gave my life to you and accepted you as my Savior, yet I am a failure, a horrible mother and awful wife. I have no faith that my life is going to get better!**

This is the cry of many hearts today. You thought you had your life all figured out. You had dreams, goals and a clear direction for your life. But yet along the way you have faced nothing but upsets, disappointments, and despair. When you were younger you had so much energy and optimism. You started out with great passion and enthusiasm for life. You may have spent years trying to climb the proverbial corporate ladder, chasing a childhood dream or trying to start your own business, only to be rejected, have doors slammed shut in your face, looked over, or discriminated against.

Ten or more so years later you find yourself at the end of your own strength. You have allowed anger, bitterness, and despondency to become the lords of your life. Although you may have accepted Christ into your life, you still feel helpless and hopeless. Every area of your life is broken and you have come to the realization that *you* are the common denominator. You have let years of discouragement, failure, and defeat beat down your door. Maybe you have lost all hope and cannot possibly fathom a better life for yourself.

Have you ever considered that perhaps God has brought you to your end so that He can give you a new beginning in Him? Perhaps He has allowed you to wear yourself out in order for you to renew your strength in Him. Perhaps He is directing your steps so you can have a *full* life in Him, as opposed to the half of a life you would create for yourself! Beloved, this crossroad is where many make the wrong turn and walk out of Jesus' path. In the book of Acts, after God chastised Paul (then named Saul) because of his persecution of Christians, He gave Ananias a vision and sent him to Paul to speak the word of the Lord concerning Paul's life (Acts 9:10-18). In verse 13, Ananias answered, "Lord I have heard from many about this man, how much harm he has done to your saints in Jerusalem." The Bible says that the Lord told Ananias that Paul is a chosen vessel and that he will bear "My name." Moreover, the Lord professed, **"For I will show him how many things he must suffer for My name's sake." Acts 9:16.**

After Ananias laid hands on Paul, the scales fell off his eyes and he was filled with the Holy Spirit. Beloved, God not only opened Paul's natural eyes, but his spiritual eyes as well! His soul was set afire for the teaching of Christ! So much so that after Paul's conversion on the road of Damascus, he traveled to different regions to establish the Gospel of Jesus Christ. One such place was Thessalonica. It was out of Paul's own oppression and

Christian persecution, that the letter to the Thessalonians was written. In 1 Thessalonians 3:3, Paul says **"that no one should be shaken by these afflictions; for you yourselves know that we are appointed for this."** In the letter, Paul reminds them of the time he visited them and told them that Christ's followers will have to suffer tribulation, and now that revelation had indeed come to pass!

When God called Paul out of a sinful and rebellious life, He clearly told him that he would have to endure many hardships on his new journey. However, when Paul accepted God's invitation and was filled with the Holy Spirit, that allotted him boldness and courage to defeat the enemies that would come before him. Many of you may have started out like Paul on the road to Damascus: full of hate, judgment, bitterness, and autonomy. You may have let wrong thinking direct your life, and because of it you have become your own worst enemy! Many people are living powerless and defeated simply because they have not appointed Christ as their Godhead, and have not claimed their power and authority in Him! Paul's letters still apply to you today, he warns that as Christians you will be afflicted for the gospel's sake, but saints it's Christ that will give you the strength to overcome any trial you face. Tap into His power and defeat your enemies!

Matthew 11:12 says, **And from the days of John the Baptist until now, the kingdom of Heaven suffers violence, and the violent take if by force**

(NHEB).

Beloved, that means that a violent war is raging against heaven, and we as Christ's saints must rise up aggressively and attack our enemies. We must not just lay down and let our enemy ransack our homes and destroy our families. No! We must use our spiritual sword and go to battle! A lazy Christian is a defeated one!

Repeat this prayer:

Holy spirit, I ask you to come into my heart and lead me. I release the spirits of negative thinking, defeat, failure and self-destruction right now. Give me discernment in the spirit realm, and help me to have courage and boldness in You, in Jesus' name. Amen!

Beloved, if you are to be triumphant in this Christian life, you must have boldness and courage! To proclaim victory over any area of your life, first you must start by winning the war that is raging against yourself! Begin to believe that *you are strong*, *you are a winner* and not a loser, and *you can overcome* anything that life throws your way! You have to turn your victim mentality into a *victor* mentality! Whatever darts satan throws at you, you can render them powerless by standing your ground, stated in Ephesians 6:14. You must train yourself to be on guard and to be vigilant against satan's evil devices. Ephesians 6:12, reminds us that **"...we wrestle not against flesh and blood, but against**

principalities, against powers, against the rulers of the darkness of this world, against spiritual wickedness in high places!"

Don't be your own worst enemy by beating yourself up, putting yourself down, treating yourself badly, feeling discouraged and helpless. You will have already lost the battle to yourself before you even begin to fight your enemies! People will treat you as well as you treat yourself! Command your respect and dignity! No matter what situation you are going through, or how many times you get knocked down, get back up again, get back in the race. Keep going, keep trying until you succeed! You have God on your side, You are more than a conqueror!

Romans 8:37-39

Yet in all these things we are more than conquerors through Him who loves us. For I am persuaded that neither death nor life, nor angels nor principalities nor powers, nor things present nor things to come, nor height nor depth, nor any other created thing, shall be able to separate us from the love of God which is in Christ Jesus our Lord.

Does Persecution Mean God Is Punishing Me?

If you are living according to the mandates of the Holy Bible and are being persecuted, it's because you are an effective witness for the Lord Jesus Christ. Contrarily, those that are sitting comfortable in the Lord, satan doesn't want to bother them. He sees them sitting perched high on their religious chair, not ministering to anybody, not praying—let alone praying for others—not reading their Bible, not serving God's kingdom. Their ministry is their lip service: "God is good all the time!" Or, "I'm blessed, sanctified, and filled with the Holy Ghost!" Oh, satan's going to leave that one alone. When saved people are complacent they are doing the devil's work for him by being immobile. He tricks them and makes them think everything's going good in their lives and builds them up in false pride. He gets them really comfortable in life so he can get them to a place of compromise. When things are going good for most people, if they aren't careful, they may slowly start entertaining things they previously walked away from.

Satan will entice them, he whets their appetite by dangling worldly carrots in front of their eyes: notoriety, sex, money and material possessions. "Sure, you can have extravagant prosperity, act like the world, dress like the world, talk like the world, watch porn, party, drink, smoke, have sex; even with somebody else's husband or wife," satan will tell them. He will have them so comfortable in him until they start believing his lies! He will have adulterers breaking marriage covenants, rationing in their mind, "This is my soulmate, God put us together." In their heart they remember the word of

God, but out of selfish desire they let satan lead them by their emotions, by their wants, lusts, and the secret desires of their heart. Slowly, he pulls them back on his side. But the best part about it for him is, not only has he lured them away from God, he now has them calling themselves a "Christian," and going to church doing his work for him! He is now using them as his puppet to blind, destroy and desensitize souls that God is trying to reach, by their amoral lifestyle. Non-Christians look at these type of people and say, **"They get drunk, shack up before marriage, and go to the same night clubs I go to, so why should I follow God?" Some others will say, "Okay well it looks like I don't have to give up anything to become a Christian; sign me up!"**

When you compromise, you are causing the people who are watching you utter confusion, and you are leading them further away from Christ! It may be your children, your drug relapsed sibling, your Christian doubting mother, or a promiscuous friend. You are misrepresenting Christianity by telling those watching you a spiritual lie: that you can have the world and God at the same time! Many who compromise, have huge houses, drive expensive cars, and are well-off financially. Foolishly, most people relate material success as the only way to be blessed by God. They don't know the compromises that are being made behind closed doors! If any of the above situations apply to you, I implore you to get right with God. Sooner or later, the sin you're involved in will catch up to you! The Bible says pride goes before destruction, and a haughty spirit before fall (Proverb 16:18). 2 Corinthians 6:17, warns to,**"Come out from among them, and be separate, says the Lord. Do not touch what is unclean, and I will receive you."**

Moreover, Christians who are on fire for the Lord may be ridiculed by and talked about in the church: "Oh they think they are Paul with all of that preaching and ministering! It don't take all of that!" Yet these same people wonder why God isn't using them. They see how God's hand is moving powerfully in the person's life, but because of their lack of power they belittle the person. To get that power you've got to suffer, you've got to go through some things, you've got to know what it feels like to be so hungry that your stomach feels like it's eating your insides! I tell you, you've got to know what it's like to go into the prayer closet in the morning and not come out until late at night. The same people complaining about the person's fire for God, turn right around and disparage the faithful Christian when they go through a trial, "If they were living right and doing God's will they wouldn't be persecuted. They must be sinning because they are always going through something." Society now has a distorted view of how God blesses people. It has deduced God's favor to merely material possessions and monetary gain. **Christians throughout the world, some living in the most desolate countries, are richly blessed with God's peace, joy, and love**, but are some of the poorest people on earth. These faithful hearts are serving God without compromising. When you stand firm for God and do not bend for the world, beloved you will suffer. People will dislike you, ridicule you because of this gospel you are proclaiming, and viciously hate you! We are living in a time when society is trying to erase Christ from all areas of life! That's why He says in Luke 22:32: **"I have prayed for you that your faith won't fail."** He knows that this path is going to be excruciatingly hard. But God is training soldiers! God has to allow you to go through certain battles to train your spiritual muscles. Oftentimes, He will have to bring you through before you can get a *Breakthrough!* You will go through many trials because you are a threat to satan; because you are not compromising! Those sold out for Christ are praying souls out of his hand. Their ministry is breaking the shackles of sin, loosing the bonds of wickedness, feeding the bread of life to a starving and malnourished generation.

And you wonder why *you* are being persecuted? This Christianity was built on the blood of persecution. God will allow persecution for every Christian that desires to know *His* will for his or her life. He uses it to establish a deeper relationship with Him and understanding of Him. God has to allow you to go through the billows of life in order for you to know for yourself that *He is real*. Pain is what often draws us to Christ. Persecuted people who continue to fight the good fight for God are a threat to the kingdom of darkness! Satan pursues them because they are taking souls from his kingdom. He's trying to shut the mouth of God's people with poverty, attacks, tribulation, war, and suffering. But the more he attacks, the more he's helping to further spread the gospel because when God's people are attacked, they're driven to their knees to seek the heart of God. Oh, but when they get back up, Isaiah 40:31 says, **But those who wait on the Lord shall renew their strength; they shall mount up with wings like eagles, They shall run and not be weary, They shall walk and not faint.**

Satan's attacks are only creating testimonies, bringing resistant souls to Christ by the miracles that's being performed in lieu of attacks, and creating a "fire" in those hungry for Christ. God commands us in Mark 16:16, **to go into all the world and preach the gospel to every creature.** Complacency should not be commonplace in the kingdom of God. If you are lukewarm, I ask you to reexamine your relationship with Christ. Ask Him to give you a fresh outpouring, a new anointing of the Holy Spirit. So many people have been hurt and turned off by the so-called "church."

Beloved, there are souls that are desperate and hungry for the pure word of God. They are seeking Christians who will walk upright and uphold their integrity regarding the things of God. They are tired of being mislead. They seek a people who will speak the truth according to the Holy Bible and live according to its doctrine. Let your life serve as light on a high tower, beaming ever so brightly to those who are perishing in darkness.

The Valley Of The Shadow Of Death

The word of God teaches you how to fight. When you face trials and tribulation, you will either succumb to the attack or put on your God appointed armor and go to battle! *Caveat Emptor:* It requires courage! Just face it now, if you're born again and you choose the call of **The Great Commission,** you will face a life-long spiritual battle with the devil! The life of Christianity is not passive. It is not sitting still, desperately hoping for the battle to be over; but contrarily, it is picking up your spiritual weapons and taking back the ground the enemy has stolen from you! So many Saints are passive and allow their most valuable possessions to be taken away from them: Their marriage, children, career, happiness; and subsequently endure a life of harassment, mental torment and persecution from the devil. Health, joy and peace can be yours, but you've got to fight for it! If only you will have courage and step forward in faith. Stand firmly on God's promises and make up your mind that *you are* a fighter, and *you will* take back ground stolen from you, your family members and loved ones; precious lives the enemy has destroyed.

The thief does not come except to steal, and to kill, and to destroy. I have come that they may have life, and that they may have it more abundantly (John 10:10).

Beloved, one must be spiritually prepared, and not blindly step on spiritual landmines set by the enemy to destroy you! What are those landmines? Demonic influences in your home, in your social life, when you travel, your business dealings, your finances, and your health! Satan works through people! Sometimes the attacks are so vicious it may feel like bombs are exploding all around you! More, some battles you will lose! But it's for God appointed reasons. Others you may have to keep fighting a lifetime, and it may seem like the enemy is not budging!

There was a beloved pastor's wife whom I knew of. This beautiful, humble soul was stricken with cancer at an early age. It was reported that she had suffered twenty-one or so grueling surgeries! One can barley tolerate the thought of one surgery let alone twenty-one! Sadly to report, after many decades of her crying out in prayer, and the church interceding in prayer on her behalf, the First Lady eventually lost her battle to cancer. Some things we will just have to endure that only God knows the answers to. But, we must not lose hope! It will take persistence, consistency, and endurance to keep going in this race! When severe pressure is upon us, hard as it may be, we must not cave in and quit or give up. Even when you feel like you can't pray, God knows your thoughts before you even think them–keep your mind on Him! When you feel like you can't read your Bible, turn on worship music and let the words minister to your spirit! Remembering:

Weeping may endure for a night, but joy cometh in the morning (Psalm 30:5 KJV). You cannot give up!

The "night" matures you spiritually, it makes you more Christ like. When you first gave your life to Christ, there may have been overwhelming joy and great anticipation of your new Christian walk: you joined a church, attended new believer's classes and were supplied Christian books to read. There was a general feeling of well-being that you were finally on the right path in life. You felt God's hand upon your life because He delivered you out of deep bondage. But further along on your Christian journey, you began to face situations that challenged your faith, situations that tested your will, situations that you couldn't find the answers to in a self-help book. My friend, you may have experienced devastating, life altering situations that knocked you down to the floor–literally. Situations that resigned you to a fetal position as you wept like a baby. When life knocks you down, that's the perfect position to pray and cry out to God! Beloved, this may have been your "night," but the Bible says that if you will just trust in Him with *all* your heart and *all* your mind *(Proverbs 3:5)*, your joy will come in the morning! Amen!

There are different stages of our Christian walk. After conversion, you first learn how pray, how to maneuver the Bible, and what it means to live a God-called life. Secondly, God then begins to show you what your calling is in Him. Along with that calling, rest assured, will come an assigned fleet of demons whose job it is to do everything in their power to disprove the anointing God put on your life! The next phase will be the testing of your will and your faith. Indeed, the hardest stage for the called in Christ! In this stage you will experience extreme torment from the devil, even though you may be doing all the spiritual work! For those who may be saying, "This isn't my testimony," this message is not for you! This message is for those on the front lines of spiritual warfare, those who are experiencing extreme harassment from the devil because of their anointed call in Christ! The devil vehemently hates it when another God appointed pastor is birthed, another church is planted, and when another sinner gives his soul to Christ! You will go through periods when God's voice will seem reticent, or you may question God's loyalty. It will seem as if all hell has broken loose in every area of your life! You will be persecuted on every side, and may feel as Paul did on his Christian journey:

For even when we came into Macedonia, our bodies had no rest, but we were afflicted at every turn–fighting without and fear within (2 Corinthians 7:5).

It may seem as if you are screaming out to God with all your might and yet your voice is inaudible. You may even become angry at God in His silence. It's a time of testing, tearing down, building up, and strengthening you. It will cause you to go deeper into the work of Christ: deeper in study, deeper in spiritual preparation, deeper in prayer and deeper in fasting. His silence is teaching you how to adamantly trust the word of God and not your feelings! No matter how dark the valley is, He's teaching you to fear not the evil one. He's teaching you that, although you cannot see Him or feel His presence, He's fighting right along side you! It's like the parable of the footsteps in the sand; you will look back and wonder in amazement, how you made it through! Amen! It's because God carried you! We were wounded and ready to be slaughtered, yet a loving Savior picked us up when our strength failed and carried us the rest of the way! Selah!

The longer it takes you to completely trust and have faith in God, I believe the longer your spiritual growth will be stunted in your Christian walk. Christianity requires proactively growing in Christ. There will be trial and error in your learning yes, but to grow in Him with a purpose and a plan, that requires diligent study, prayer, and a concerted effort to make time with God daily. Beloved, there is something to be said about spending time in God's presence. The anointing comes down! There is a sweet peace. God will give you wisdom and knowledge, and He will perform signs and wonders! He will tell you secrets, give you direction and ideas your mind could never have possibly conceived on its own.

And by the hands of the apostles were many signs and wonders wrought among the people; and they were all with one accord in Solomon's porch (Acts 5:12 KJV).

In the latter part of your Christian walk, you may enter into a place of supernatural discernment. You will be given godly wisdom, knowledge and a deeper understanding of spirituality! Those called began to teach, edify, encourage, heal, prophesy, speak and interpret tongues among other gifts *(1 Corinthians 12:4-12)*. There will still be testing, but it will not destroy you like it used to! You'll know the exact spiritual tools needed to apply against your enemy and come out a victor! Amen! You will have a concrete belief in God; no trick, lie, or scheme from the devil will be able to dissuade you. You will know that it's a war between good and evil, and you will distinctively know your place in the battle. You will know that silence does not mean neglect. You will know that you and God are in this together!

Humbly, the valley experience will change your attitude! You may have walked with Christ for years but still have a defeated mentality! Instead of thinking you are a defeater and knowing that you are already equipped to win the fight raged against you *(Luke 10:19)*, you are numb because of persecution, and are thinking defeated thoughts. To live a victorious life in Christ, there has to be a turning over of subdued mental thinking to the side of victory. Your spiritual language has to change. You have to learn to always speak positive words over your life and circumstances no matter what your physical eyes may be showing you. You have to learn how to see with your spiritual eyes–the eyes of faith!

Additionally, your mindset has to change. A lot of people may quote Biblical verses and say all the popular Christian slogans, but deep down inside, perhaps because of continuous oppression, have not come to a place where they believe what they are actually saying! The opposition can be so intense that you have given up emotionally! You're spiritually dead! You have been sowing, but sadly feel like you are not reaping. It's a testing beyond your toughest strength! With all your might and knowledge about God, you've got to take Him at His word; getting into your spirit man the living word of God!

For the word of God is quick, and powerful, and sharper than any two-edged sword, piercing even to the dividing asunder of soul and spirit, and of the joints and marrow, and is a discerner of the thoughts and intents of the heart (Hebrews 4:12 KJV).

People often talk about knowing God's character. What exactly is the character of God? It is the culmination of His teachings, His finished work through the lives of Biblical prophets, and His grace. The devil tries to undermine God and His work in your life. Fight hard with all that is within you to not believe him! We are living in an evil, vile, more diabolical spiritual atmosphere in this day and time. Satan's kingdom has become more perverted and more wicked. Its mission is not the ungodly–he already has them under his control–but specifically to attack the saints of God and the church! The death in the valley is so gruesome beloved, let us not forget the saints that are literally fighting a battle with the devil; those that daily face harassment, suffering and torment because they live in countries that do not tolerate Christianity; those who have lost their lives for the sake of the Gospel! We're seeing more and more today, persecution against those who live in established countries. They are being harassed and ostracized; their businesses threatened because of their Christian belief. All in the vein of political correctness. As we continue to carry the weight of our cross–with hardships, burdens and tears–let us remember: the battle is not between us and the devil, but between God and satan!

Yea, though I walk through the valley of the shadow of death, I will fear no evil: for thou art with me; thy rod and thy staff they comfort me (Psalm 23:4).

The Red Pumps

As I walked into the store, it was abuzz, a frenzy, a free for all! The floor was cluttered with shoes, shoes, and more shoes!: *Nine West, Steve Madden, Coach*—the list was endless! It was shoe heaven! There were mounds of high heels, boots, flats, open-toed, pointy, black, white, yellow, green—any style or color, you name it, they had it! Women soldiers were everywhere, staking their claim! As I scoped things out, I was preparing myself to join in the shoe battle—take no prisoners! It was a pair of turquoise, snakeskin, high heels—oh so beautifully perched in the store's window—that stopped me dead in my tracks; and like the serpent in the Garden of Eden, deceptively lured me inside the forbidden store! (I was disciplining myself in the area of shopping).

As I went over to touch them, I hear, " Don't even think about it!" hurdle past me along with flying shoes being jostled about by a mob of aggressive shoe nazi's at the close out sale. Right then, a lady with about five pairs of loot stashed in a corner, snatched them away just like that! It was rough, it was tough, it was shoe hysteria! You had to fight your way through the horde to get to the stash. So, I stepped back, rolled up my sleeves, took a deep breath and I went in...R-A-M-B-O! I was in for the fight of my *shoe* life: there was pushing, shoving, bumping, but I was not to be deterred—you can't separate a woman from her shoes! I was grabbing, reaching, pulling—*Shoot! wrong size, no match, wrong color; throw back, damaged, too high, too gaudy.* I finally worked my way into the enemy's camp—the lady who was hoarding all the best shoes—and started exploiting her territory! I'm grabbing, digging, bargaining and coming up with nothing! *Sigh...these shoes are at rock bottom prices, surely there must be at least one pair for me!* I was getting nowhere but overwhelmed. I retorted to plan B: spy on another nemesis with a hand full of eye candy and raid her territory! *Voila!*...I spotted my target–*Y*es! I moved in covertly as she was admiring a lovely pair of red pumps.

I anxiously awaited the drop. Patiently plotting on the sideline for its release back into the shoe abyss. OK, she's trying them on...*waiting*...she's walking around in them...*waiting*...she's heading towards the cash register. *Oh no! She's going to buy them?!* Not to fret, the conqueror in me was not succumbing; I held my undercover post (begging in prayer), *Lord, please don't let her buy those shoes!* It took a moment, then f*inally!;* another pair caught her eye and she dropped them! I hurriedly snatched them up! They were perfect! Actually, I had been trying to find a pair of red pumps for awhile. As I more closely examined one of the shoes, I noticed there was a flaw. One side of the shoe was slightly scuffed, but hey, nothing a shoe tailor couldn't fix! Alas! I had found my perfect pair of shoes! You know, *Habakkuk 3:19,* did say *"...He will make me walk on my high hills."* Ok!...ok!..I know He wasn't talking about those high heels.

On the way out of the store a very interesting thought came to me. Out of all the piles of name brand, new shoes, the defective ones were the pair that I loved the most and were the most perfect for me. It reminded me of how Christ loves us! Even though you may have been damaged and used up by this world, and may have gone astray in pursuit of your own interests and desires, God still chases after you! His grace is so magnificent in that out of the remaining ninety-nine, He went after the one lost sheep. *(Matt 18:12).*

Just as He chose us in him before the foundation of the world, that we should be holy and without blame before Him in love, having predestined us to adoption as sons by Jesus Christ to Himself, according to the good pleasure of His will, to the praise of the glory of His grace, by which He made us accepted in the beloved. Ephesians 1:4-6.

Beloved, He loves us and chose us as His own, despite our short comings and transgressions. There is nothing we have to do to receive Christ's love but accept it by grace.

Accepting Jesus as your personal Savior

Maybe you have heard people talk about salvation in Jesus Christ, or you are currently reading this book but don't know him personally as your savior. Or, perhaps Christians have approached you on the street trying to hand you a Bible tract, but you just don't know...you've contemplated this *Jesus thing* but are afraid that you'll have to give up too much of your life or give up having fun. Today, I extend to you His invitation! More, maybe you have family members or loved ones who don't know Christ, the following is a guideline to use to introduce them to Jesus. To accept Christ as your personal Savior, all you have to **confess, believe** and **receive** Him!

CONFESS:

Romans 10:9

Says that if you *confess* with your mouth the Lord Jesus and believe in your heart that God has raised Him from the dead, you will be saved.

Sinner's Prayer (Repeat this prayer aloud):

Heavenly Father, I come to you in prayer today asking for forgiveness for my sins. I confess with my mouth and believe in my heart that Jesus Christ is the Son of God and that He died on the cross so that I might be forgiven and have eternal life. I believe that He rose from the grave and granted me the assistance of the

Holy Spirit to help me. I accept Him into my heart right now to be my personal savior. I repent of my sins and confess with my mouth that I am cleansed by the blood of The Lamb. In Jesus' name I pray, amen!

You are now a born again Christian! Hallelujah! Or, if you are ministering to people for their salvation, have them recite *your own version* of this prayer!

BELIEVE:

John 3:16

For God so loved the world that He gave His only begotten Son, that whosoever *believes* in Him shall not perish But have everlasting life.

God sent His son down to earth to die on the cross for you and me as atonement for our sins. Moreover, that if we, by faith, believe in Him we shall not die in our sins, but because of God's grace we will have everlasting life in eternity with Him.

Romans 3:25-26

Whom God set forth as a propitiation by His blood, through faith, to demonstrate His righteousness, because in His forbearance God had passed over the sins that were previously committed, to demonstrate at the present time His righteousness, that He might be just and the

justifier of the one who has faith in Jesus.

RECIEVE:

Beloved, after you have given your life to Christ, you must *receive* His will and *leading* for your life. You must allow Him to be Lord and Master over your life. Your prayer should be:

Lord, guide me in your truth and teach me, for you are God my Savior, and my hope is in you all day long. Psalm 25:5 NIV.

And hereby we do know that we know Him if we keep his commandments (1 John 23).

And do not present your members as instruments of unrighteousness unto sin, but present yourselves to God as being alive from the dead, and your members as instruments of righteousness to God (Romans 6:13).

Now that you know why Jesus died for you, by faith invite Him to be Lord over your life! But first you must equip yourself for the battle!

Christian tools:

As a babe in Christ *i.e.* a new Christian, the following are pertinent tools you will need to be effective in your Christian walk. I will also list scriptures for you to meditate on and study.

1. Warfare Verses

As stated throughout this book, praying is the most important aspect of a Christian's life, however there are many believers who simply do not pray or neglect to spend time with God. Prayer is the Christian's life line, our direct connection to God. To be victorious in Christianity one must develop the daily habit of talking to God. Without it we are weak, defenseless, and can exhort no power over the enemy, or anything else for that matter! How much more effective when you incorporate warfare verses! Warfare prayers are our spiritual weapons to defeat the powers of darkness, as well as petition God for friends, family, co-workers, the lost, as well as cry out to God for our own personal needs. Praying warfare verses is your daily protection against spiritual attacks. The first prayer all newly converted Christians must learn is ***The Lord's Prayer.*** Everyone should pray this prayer before they talk to God:

Matthew 6:9-13 (KJV)

After this manner therefore pray ye: **Our Father which art in heaven, Hallowed be thy name. Thy kingdom come, Thy will be done in earth, as it is in heaven. Give us this day our daily bread. And forgive us our debtors. And lead us not into temptation, but deliver us from evil: For thine is the kingdom, and the power, and the glory, for ever. Amen!**

The second warfare prayer that a new convert *must* learn is Psalm 23. There will be many tough challenges as a new Christian. It is of utmost importance that you memorize this verse and keep it hidden in your heart when trying times come. As well, parents this and the aforementioned are the first two verses of scripture that you must teach your children when they become of age!

Psalms 23 (KJV)

The LORD is my shepherd; I shall not want. He maketh me to lie down in green pastures: He leadeth me beside the still waters. He restoreth my soul: He leadeth me in the paths of righteousness for His name's sake. Yea, though I walk through the valley of the shadow of death, I will fear no evil: for thou art with me; thy rod and thy staff they comfort me. Thou preparest a table before me in the presence of mine enemies: thou anointest my head with oil: my cup runneth over. Surely goodness and mercy

shall follow me all the days of my life: and I will dwell in the house of the Lord for ever.

The third prayer I recommend you to pray is the ***Prayer of Jabez***. It is important to pray the Prayer of Jabez daily to petition God's protection and to proclaim His blessings over your life. The Bible says that Jabez's mother named him as such because she bore him in sorrow.

1 Chronicles 4:9-10 (NIV)

And Jabez called on the God of Israel, saying, **"Oh that you would bless me and enlarge my territory! Let your hand be with me, and keep me from harm so that I will be free from pain."**

2. Bible Reading

Bible reading is the second most important aspect of a Christian's life. In prayer we talk to God. In Bible reading God talks to us. The Bible is our compass and roadmap. It lists instructions on how we are to live our lives as Christ followers in a sinful world. More importantly, the Bible will be your greatest encourager when you face difficult times in your life. It's a good idea to have a note pad, highlighter, and a pen present when you read/study the Bible to take notes and highlight favorite scriptures, so you can always come back to them in a time of need.

Bible verses to study:

Psalm 1:2   Mark 11:23-24

Psalm 119:38 John 15:7

Psalm 119:97 Matthew 5:6

Matthew 6:33 Ephesians 6:18

Colossians 4:2

3. Fasting

Moses fasted forty days on Mount Sinai and received the Ten Commandments on stone tablets, written by the finger of God. The tablets contained the covenant law that God ordained for the Children of Israel (Deuteronomy 9:9-10). Moses, after coming down from the mountain learned of the children of Israel worshipping a molded calf and threw the tablets to the ground. Greatly grieved, he then went on another 40-day fast (Deu 9:16-18). The Bible also mentions several Biblical figures fasting at times of distress, anguish, or when needing an answer from the Lord. **Queen Esther** proclaimed a three-day fast for the salvation of her people after Haman sent out a written decree for all Jews to be killed (Esther 4:16). **Jesus** fasted 40 days in the wilderness when satan tried to tempt him (Matt 4:1-2). **Daniel** went on a 21-day fast because he did not want to defile himself with the King's royal food (Daniel 1:8-14). **David** fasted, pleading with God to save his sick son he conceived with Uriah's wife (2 Samuel 12:16).

Fasting is the denying of fleshly desires to enter into a deeper level of communication with God. A seasoned faster may fast as many as forty days or more ingesting no food or drinks. Some only fast on water or juice. Others fast eating only one meal a day, or some people may fast from sun up to sun down. Fasting is subjective to your own personal spiritual level. The more you fast the better you will become at it and you will be able to go on longer fasts. It is good to go on a fast if you need a habit broken: smoking, drug addiction, over eating, or drinking. Many people have reported success in these areas as a result of fasting combined with prayer. It is also a great time to fast when you need to hear from the Lord regarding a pressing situation in your life, if you are facing sickness or stress, or as proxy for a wayward loved one.

Fasting Bible verses to study:

Psalm 69:10

Psalm 109:24

Matthew 17:21

Mark 2:18

Mark 9:29

2 Corinthians 6:5

4. **Tithing**

Tithing should be a Christian's obligation. It is not just about giving your hard earned money to a church, but if you worship at a church that has out reach programs, or a church that funds missionary organizations, you are monetarily helping to provide for the less fortunate. A great verse regarding tithing is Deuteronomy 26:1-4, it talks about God giving his people land, and that as servants, we are to bring our first harvest before the Lord's altar. Nehemiah 10:35-38, also talks about bringing all of the first fruits of the harvest to God. Verse 38, mentions the Levites specifically bringing a "tenth" of tithes to "the house of our God." Giving should not be your aim in order that you may receive, however I do believe as Luke 6:38 says, that with the same measure that you use it will be measured back to you. More, Malachi 3:10, says "bring your tithes into the store house and see won't I open the windows of Heaven and pour you out a blessing!"

Tithing Bible verses to study:

2 Corinthians 9:7

Romans 12:8

Leviticus 27:30

Deuteronomy 14:28

Romans 12:8

5. **Communion**

Also as a new believer in Christ, you will take communion with other believers at your local church usually once a month. Communion is mentioned in the Bible as **The Lord's Supper**. The passage is as follows:

Matthew 26:26-28

While they were eating, Jesus took a piece of bread, gave a prayer of thanks, broke it, and gave it to his disciples. "Take and eat it," He said; "This is my body." Then He took a cup, gave thanks to God, and gave it to them. "Drink it, all of you," he said; this is my blood, which seals God's covenant, my blood poured out for many for the forgiveness of sins.

If you are a new covert, welcome to the brotherhood! If you are a seasoned Christian, I pray that the information in this chapter will greatly help you on your spiritual journey. God bless you, and it is my hope that you will be truly fulfilled and rewarded in your Christian walk with the Lord.

On The Road To Salvation

Throughout the course of your life, your direction will constantly change. You will swerve in and out of lanes of despair, make wrong turns on streets of failure, be grid-locked by disappointments, and get lost on the side street of delay. Life is indeed one long, winding, twisting, and arduous road; albeit, if you have given your life to Christ, God will allow *life accidents* in order to get you to relinquish your control to trust His will and guidance for your life.

No matter how daunting life's challenges along the way, God will give you the strength to keep on going in Him, and not allow you to die on the side of despair's road, however long you may be parked there from time to time. The side of the road is a place to rest awhile: to recharge your battery with prayer, receive a spiritual tune-up, and get the lamp of your spirit reignited with fresh oil to help you navigate through the darkness!

From the day we were born, we set out on a spiritual journey, with only God knowing our final destination. Onto the road of life we go; rife with love, joy, hurt, pain, sadness, loss, rebirth, and lots of learning along the way.

Ecclesiastes 3:1-8, **says there is a season and a time to every purpose under Heaven.** Some of us will drive at a much slower pace, while some of us will speed fast ahead. That's ok! Your final destination will be your own personal legacy that you have left behind; so you must continue to focus and stay in your own lane, no matter how long it may take you to get there. Rest assured, God has an appointed plan for your collisions, roadblocks, detours, and wrong turns.

We each have our own cross to bear. For some it may be sicknesses, addiction, a handicap, poverty, homelessness or imprisonment; for others it may be a lifelong battle with depression, anger, physical or sexual abuse, or mental/emotional problems. The previously mentioned could be a direct result of willing sin, having been born into it, or it may be a generational curse. Through the avenues mentioned in this book, many have received deliverance! However, there are many others who are struggling with a life time of afflictions, and detrimentally, they feel like there is no hope for them. Some have prayed, fasted, got delivered from sin but went back into bondage; they did all the spiritual work and still aren't free. Perhaps you are one of them? The pain is so intense that you feel like you don't want to live anymore. Your prayer is, "Lord, just take me today, I am ready to go!" You read all of the books on faith, went to healing ministries, and still aren't totally delivered yet! This very message is for you!

MY TESTIMONY

There I was, lifeless! I had no pulse, and my spirit wavered on the borderline of life and death's plane. My heart stopped beating, I was declared clinically dead! But God!

I was one that suffered persecution early on in life. In childhood I was plagued with debilitating sickness, learning disabilities, phobias, mental abuse, child abuse, physical abuse, child molestation, rape, alcoholism, and emotional abandonment. You see, the devil tried to run me off the road, but God said it's not my time to go! The devil tried to put my lights out, but God said, **"I am the light of the world. Whoever follows me will never walk in darkness (John 8:12)."** And that, **"A town built on a hill cannot be hidden (Matt 5:14)."** The devil tried to kill me, But God said, **"I shall not die, but live and declare the works of the Lord! (Psalm 118:17).**

Beloved, when you have a call on your life, the devil knows it too! He will start attacking you as early as in your mother's womb! He will torment, harass, plague and even try to abort you; all so he can try to deter your walk in God. If you are on the front lines with God, expect extreme persecution, suffering, opposition, rejection, even murder! Lest you forget the story of Job! The devil hates God and is trying to stop God's ministry from manifesting through you!

As I lay there on that hospital bed, wavering in and out of consciousness, my heavy eyelids slowly lowered, shutting out the noise of the world. I felt ethereal, as if I were in a deep, peaceful sleep. I saw no bodily figure, angels or visions. Oh, how I wanted to remain there and never wake up! God said: get up my child, for there is more work for you to do! And, Just like that I awoke and my heart started beating again!

I got back into my car of life and continued on my journey! Day-by-day, mile-by-mile, I travel on; stopping at a rest stop ever so often to fuel up on the *Living Water.*

Beloved, this road gets hard, dark, and lonely. Many times you may want to give up; give up on yourself, your dreams, your goals, even on life. We must continue to remind ourselves, this is not our journey: but God's! We must pick up our cross–heavy as it may be–put it in our back and follow Him! Don't give up! For He says that those who endure to the end will be saved (*Matthew 24:13).*

Keep going! Rest a moment if you have to, but get back on the road! With all of the world's evil, take heart; for stretches of miles there will be flowers blooming along the side of your road, God's *Son* shining brightly on you each day, and beautiful sunny blue skies to cheer your weeping face. From time to time, God will send you a travel companion to help you along your way. Although, you may be tempted to get upset when they leave, don't! They were only sent for an appointed time and season. For some are angels unaware (*Hebrews 13:2*).

Just keep on driving. On your journey God will allow accidents and breakdowns to get you to stop and help others along their way! It's all a part of His divine plan! If we just keep on driving, we will reach our destination whether in this life or in Heaven!

From God, with love

Beloved, I have heard the cries of your heart. Because of your recent tragedy you are now calling out to me. You have been asking where am I? But beloved, I pardon, where were you when I tried to call you unto me (Luke 5:32)? In bitter weeping I cried out to you to turn from your wicked ways. Where were you when I needed you to do my will? You turned your back on me when I tried to awake you at various times to spend time with me and pray. When I needed you to visit the sick, you went out partying instead. When I called you to fast you celebrated in feasting and revelry. When I spoke to you through a homeless person; I begged you for food, yet you rose up in anger, called me names and admonished me to get a job. I commanded you to love, yet you operated in hate, unforgiveness, and judgment towards your earthly sisters and brothers (Mark 12:31).

My heart bleeds at the arrogance and pride toward your fellow man. Instead of fellowshipping with me, you prefer to consume your time watching TV, engrossed in entertainment, on the internet, or with friends. My child, you take more pleasure in your worldly accomplishments and material possessions than in me; don't you know that it was I who gave it to you? Instead of bowing down to worship me, you worship mammon, cars, houses, jobs, and sadly yourself. Instead of me being the love of your life, you have reduced my love to the relationship of that of man. Don't you know that the love I have for you is everlasting (John 3:16)? You have made these things the gods of your life. You have pushed me aside for the pleasures and vanity of this world. Yet when tragedy happens, you say where is God? I then will say, '*I never knew you!*' (Matthew 7:23). Why do you call me *'Lord, Lord'*, and not do the things which I say (Luke 6:46)? How right Isaiah was when he prophesied about you! You are hypocrites; you honor me with your words, but your heart is really far away from me (Mark 7:6). Now because of this great disaster in your life you want to accuse me of not being a loving God, a faithful God, or a merciful God.

I clearly warned you not to commit idolatry, murder, lying, stealing, adultery and sexual perversion (Exodus 20:1-17). I am the same yesterday, today and forever more (Hebrews 13:8), my words do not change. Have you not learned from the children of Israel? (Deu 11:26-28). And now that this bereavement has come upon you, you cry out to me in desperation. Haven't I told you in Romans 14:11, that every knee shall bow before me, and every tongue will confess that I am God? Yet in your own self-reliance, you cursed me and told the world that there is no God! You turned many souls away from me into the hands of my enemy.

I now ask, are you willing to repent and seek me as the Lord of your life or do you just want me to fix this immediate problem? "Help me just one more time, this time I promise to serve you," you have cried out to me before. Are you now willing to turn away from your rebelliousness and willful sin? Beloved, I will always love you! But, will you now pick up your cross and follow me? (1Peter 4:2,3).

The lover of your soul,

Jesus Christ

The most beautiful people we have known are those who have known defeat, known suffering, know struggle, known loss, and have found their way out of the depths. These persons have an appreciation, a sensitivity, and an understanding of life that fills them with compassion, gentleness, and a deep loving concern. Beautiful people do not just happen.

-Elizabeth Kublet-Ross

www.ingramcontent.com/pod-product-compliance
Lightning Source LLC
Chambersburg PA
CBHW020419010526
44118CB00010B/321